PARENTING
FOR LIBERATION

THE FEMINIST PRESS
AT THE CITY UNIVERSITY OF NEW YORK
NEW YORK CITY

TRINA GREENE BROWN

PARENTING FOR LIBERATION

A Guide for Raising Black Children

Published in 2020 by the Feminist Press
at the City University of New York
The Graduate Center
365 Fifth Avenue, Suite 5406
New York, NY 10016

feministpress.org

First Feminist Press edition 2020

NoVo Foundation This book is supported in part by a grant from the NoVo Foundation.

NEW YORK STATE OF OPPORTUNITY. | Council on the Arts This book was made possible thanks to a grant from New York State Council on the Arts with the support of Governor Andrew M. Cuomo and the New York State Legislature.

Second printing May 2021

Cover design and interior art by Amir Khadar
Photos throughout by Jayia Kim
Text design by Drew Stevens

Library of Congress Cataloging-in-Publication Data is available for this title.
ISBN 978-1-936932-84-9

PRINTED IN THE UNITED STATES OF AMERICA

This book is dedicated to my daddy,
Timothy Greene
(9/20/1958–1/14/2020).
It's because of the love and power
you instilled in me that
I am the liberated parent I am.

Contents

Introduction

I n 2014, when my son was five years old, it seemed like every time I watched the news, I saw another Black person being murdered or impacted by state violence. It wasn't only adult men and women, but young Black children's lives that were (and still are) being taken by those sworn to "protect and serve." The recurring images of Black bodies left in the streets after being shot by police (such as Michael Brown, an eighteen-year-old gunned down in Ferguson, Missouri, in the summer of 2014 whose lifeless body lay in the street for four hours), coupled with the historical legacy of Black bodies hanging after lynchings, compounded my fears as a Black parent. Trayvon Martin, Jordan Davis, Aiyana Stanley-Jones, and Tamir Rice—are contemporary Emmett Tills. I became worried that I would become a modern-day Mamie Till-Mobley, a mother-turned-activist after her fourteen-year-old son, Emmett Till, was murdered in the summer of 1955 in Mississippi when Carolyn Bryant Donham falsely accused him of whistling at her. Mamie is a foremother to the many modern-day "mothers of the movement," all of whom are compelled by grief to share their children's deaths publicly with the world; it is a "club" that many Black mothers are fearful that we will be forced to join, crying over the bodies of our African American children. This fear, which is a trauma response, encourages Black parents (including me, and maybe you) to engage in parenting strategies that are detrimental to Black children, in the name of protecting them—and us.

These behaviors are rooted in what Dr. Joy DeGruy coined as *post-traumatic slave syndrome* wherein "African Americans adapted their behavior over centuries in order to survive the stifling effects of chattel slavery, effects which are evident today . . . in large part related to trans-generational adaptations associated with the past traumas of slavery and ongoing oppression." Dr. DeGruy gives an example of the survival strategies employed by enslaved mothers, such as being hypervigilant about the whereabouts of their children because it was unsafe for Black children to stray for fear of severe punishment.

Does this sound familiar to you? This dynamic has definitely been at play in my parenting practice, and it took deep self-reflection and a lot of reading to begin to unpack it. Even though my family lives in a community with an enclosed community playground, I was terrified of allowing my son, Terrence, to play outside without me being present, let alone out of my eyesight. In the fall of 2016, I hosted a Parenting for Liberation gathering on Black Friday. As parents sat in a community circle sharing our deepest fears, our children were next door dreaming up their visions of liberated lives as superheroes. At the close of the event, the parents and children came together, and as each child shared their superhero name, costume, and superpower, each parent was to make a commitment to a shift that would help to foster that superpower in their children. When Terrence shared his superpower—to teleport—it dawned on me that he wanted to have the freedom to move without constraints of time, space, or even me as his mother. I made a commitment that day—publicly—to allow Terrence more space to explore and play.

That shift came in increments. In 2017, when I finally allowed him to go outside and play without me, I required him to check in every ten minutes, with one "simple" request: "Let me know you're alive." Every ten to fifteen minutes, Terrence would run to the door and check in. What he said upon checking in made sadness rise up like a lump in my throat. My seven-year-old son would burst into our home and yell "I'm alive!" and then run back out to play.

After a while, his non-Black friends caught on and would come to the door with him, waiting for this small interruption in their playing to end. Though at the time it appeared to be a minor inconvenience, I realized I was communicating something to my son. When I saw my Black boy having to affirm his life, with his non-Black peers in the background, I realized I was reinforcing that he had to validate his right to be free and childlike. It was like his own version of declaring Black Lives Matter. The only difference was that he wasn't proclaiming this to a racist system or institution and he wasn't declaring this in the face of state violence; this proclamation was to me, his mother. He had to affirm to me that his freedom matters and his space to play and have fun matters.

I realize that the mainstream may refer to this as being a "helicopter parent." As a Black parent who is raising Black children, I did not see this as being a helicopter parent. In fact, many of us actually *are* parenting children in "helicopter environments," where our children are frequently under surveillance and their movements policed. Parenting under constant surveillance and policing places limits on the exploration, play, freedom, and free spirit of children and childhood. These conditions lead Black parents, including myself, to use harm-reduction techniques such as not allowing my children to speak up for fear of them being considered a threat; having "the talk" with my children on how to engage with police; being the "fashion police" for fear that what my child is wearing could cause deadly interaction with the police; or moving to a "better" neighborhood school because we believe education is the ultimate equalizer. Parenting from these restrictive viewpoints increases dominance over children and can lead to engaging in abusive parenting practices, such as utilizing power and control, punitive tactics, and harsh physical, verbal, and emotional punishment. In my home, I found myself clamping down on my son, saying no more than saying yes, and raising my voice. I realized that I was not living out my values of equity, joy, love, and freedom in my home because I was parenting from a place of fear. I was parenting to protect, but protection did not allow my child to be free. I was putting boundaries and restrictions on my child's humanity, and I was blocking him from being his freest self because I was afraid. I realized I wanted and needed a shift. I wanted to unlearn and heal from my fear and replace it with liberation and freedom.

In making this shift, I did an assessment of the resources and tools available for parents who are raising Black children to be free. I found online resources to engage children in conversations about race. I also found a few books and readings written by parents of color such as *Revolutionary Mothering: Love on the Front Lines*, an anthology edited by Alexis Pauline Gumbs, China Martens, and Mai'a Williams, that focuses on placing mothers of color at the center of movement building and social change, and *My Brown Baby: On the Joys and Challenges of Raising African American Children* by Denene Millner, and *Letters to My Black Sons: Raising Boys in a Post-Racial America* by Dr. Karsonya Wise Whitehead.

I realized that I was not living out my values of equity, joy, love, and freedom in my home because I was parenting from a place of fear.

While I did find some resources to equip me and other parents with the necessary skills to practice liberated parenting, I yearned for more resources that spoke directly to the unique experiences of parenting while Black. I began to reach out to my elders and peers in the social justice community to engage in dialogue about their struggles and how they made and are making the shift from fear to liberation in their own parenting practices. In my early conversations, I realized that there is a gap to be filled for myself and for other Black parents. There is a need for both resources and tools, and to be connected to each other. There is a need for parents to be in community with one another, having conversations about the day-to-day pains, struggles, joys, and hopes of raising Black children to be their freest selves.

After realizing this critical gap in resources and community for Black parents who are intentionally practicing liberation in their parenting, I created Parenting for Liberation based on my belief in the power of parents to conceive, birth, and nurture liberation for the future. Launched in 2016 as a virtual platform featuring blogs and podcasts to connect, inspire, and uplift Black parents as they navigate and negotiate raising Black children within the social and political context of the United States, Parenting for Liberation is rooted in an Afrofuturist vision of a world where Black parents are in community with each other to raise Black children without fear and instead parent for liberation. Our mission is to cultivate resilient and joyful Black families that are doing the healing work to interrupt historical traumas, dismantle harmful narratives about Black families, and create community that amplifies Black girl magic and Black boy joy and everything in between.

Our mission is to cultivate resilient and joyful Black families that are doing the healing work to interrupt historical traumas, dismantle harmful narratives about Black families, and create community that amplifies Black girl magic and Black boy joy and everything in between.

Since Parenting for Liberation's inception, I have created space to learn with and from other Black parents about what it takes to be liberated parents. Some of the engagement strategies that have grounded my work for the past couple of years have ranged from one-on-one conversations with Black parents, to large group workshops with parents and children, and sharing my learnings via writing both online and in print.

I've been in conversation with over thirty Black parents and recorded those dialogues in podcasts. I've engaged Black parents online through my blog and social media. I've had the pleasure of gathering groups of Black parents in Los Angeles, San Diego, Detroit, Chicago, Boise, and St. Helena, holding space for Black parents who are freedom fighting for their collective liberation, to engage with one another, and share how they operationalize liberation in their homes. Knowing that parenting is a collective effort, I have had incredible collaborators such as Move to End Violence, Mothering Justice, CADRE, A Long Walk Home, Black Activist Mothering, and Chicana M(other)work, with whom I have led parenting workshops in women's prisons in California and for whom I wrote a chapter in their anthology.

Through Parenting for Liberation, I work in deep partnership with Black parents to name, interrupt, and transform trauma responses as a strategy to cultivate liberated parents that are ready to challenge institutional violence and racism on behalf of their children and community.

My core belief? Centering Black parents is key to unlocking the multiple barriers to disrupting the cycles of oppression that are perpetrated against Black communities. Parenting is a political act, after all. Audre Lorde, Black queer feminist poet and scholar, described her parenting as a revolutionary act that had the ability to liberate and free not only her own children but also engage her children as agents of social change.

What is becoming clearer is the need to identify ways to shift from fear to liberation before we can activate Black parents to challenge institutional oppression. The work has evolved from focusing on ways of parenting our children to engaging with Black parents to do their own healing and transformative work and supporting Black parents to understand intergenerational trauma rooted in slavery. Based on research by Dr. Joy DeGruy, there are many chains that need to be broken to heal

Black parents from the impact of post-traumatic slave syndrome, such as punitive parenting styles, that are rooted in fear from slavery.

Rather than vilifying Black parents, Parenting for Liberation is working to unearth and connect to these deep-seated historical traumas and provide liberatory and healing practices for Black parents. When parents can access their own liberation and healing, they are equipped to advocate and support their children and community. Imagine Black parents with multiple seats at decision-making tables. The decisions and solutions conjured up in those spaces would be inherently radical, centering the most impacted and laying the foundation for equity for ourselves, in our homes, and in community.

Now, when Terrence is outside playing, he is no longer required to check in, declaring that he's alive. Instead he plays in community with other children whose parents and grandparents I've built relationships with. I have the security of knowing that I don't have to parent alone, and that there is a village of folks who are keeping an eye on him.

About This Guide

This guide is a compilation of stories collected from the podcast interview transcripts of Parenting for Liberation. Throughout the many conversations I've had with Black parents, it is becoming clear that the impact of fear and trauma is disconnection. Disconnection from self, from our children, and from community. Thus, the pathway to interrupting and healing from the trauma is *reconnection*.

This guide is broken down into three sections that highlight three paths of connection that support the shift from fear-based parenting to liberated parenting: (re)connection to self, (re)connection to our children, (re)connection to community.

Section One will highlight stories of parents who have explored the ways that we can (re)connect to ourselves such as increasing awareness of our own trauma response, exploring our own childhood trauma, identifying habits that were learned as children that we can unlearn, and exploring healing practices. Section Two will reveal stories of (re)connecting with our children by being in a mutual and equitable relationship with our children that honors their identity and their truths, exploring family practices that integrate children's voices, and the types of educational environments that will help elevate their sense of pride in self as Black children. Section Three will share stories from parents who are (re)connecting to community by building with other Black parents to share stories, swap strategies, and remind us that we are not alone, while also connecting to larger societal contexts and social justice movements.

Accompanying each story are "Liberated Parenting Strategies," which first invite you to reflect on a particular shift that you can make in your parenting followed by an opportunity to practice the strategies that are discussed in the story—what of those strategies are applicable to you and your parenting? Space is provided for your written reflections. Feel free to use other means to reflect such as art, poetry, journaling, etc.

This guide can be done individually or collectively. We know that each parent-child relationship is different and there are no one-size-fits-all guidelines for parenting. We hope that this guide inspires you on your journey toward liberatory parenting.

SECTION 1

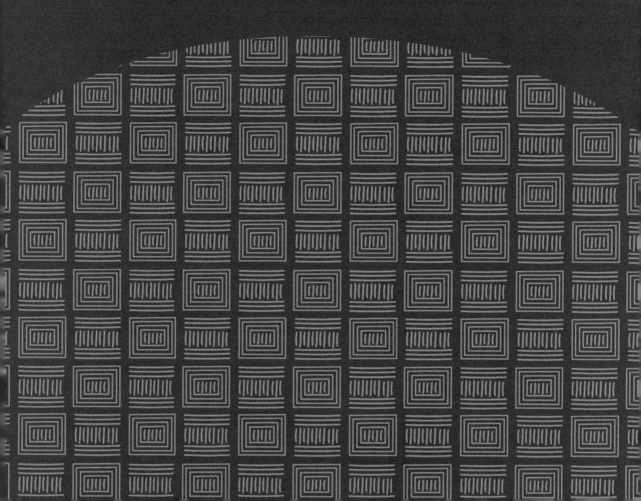

(Re)connection to Self

SECTION 1

(Re)connection to Self

Section One focuses on (re)connection with the self. Parents spend a lot of time, energy, and resources focused on their children. The first step on the path to parenting for liberation is to seize the opportunity to look at and be present to self through deep self-reflection and self-awareness. Section One provides an opportunity to look in the mirror—which can be challenging! This isn't about looking at yourself in the mirror to fixate on flaws, but to instead embrace the pieces of you that are sometimes hard to accept and loving them, still—all the places of imperfection. Once you've looked in the mirror, another element of (re)connection to self involves parenting ourselves and nurturing ourselves—essentially, giving love and attention to our own inner child.

Throughout this section, you will read stories from Black parents who have begun the hard work of self-reflection and (re)connecting with self. Stories in this section will highlight narratives of parents who have explored the ways that we can reconnect to ourselves, including increasing awareness of our own trauma responses, exploring our own childhood trauma, identifying habits that were learned as children that we can unlearn, and exploring healing practices.

Following the stories of deep self-reflection, you will be invited to do your own self-reflection through various liberated parenting strategy exercises. The exercises engage a variety of reflection approaches such as poetry, music, videos, journaling, and art. We want to invite multiple ways of learning. As you do these exercises, notice what comes up for you. Reflecting on your childhood self, what are you learning about yourself? What are you loving—or learning to love—about yourself? As you do these exercises, remember to offer grace and love to the places that may feel hard, and gratitude and celebration to the places that feel joyful.

Breaking Apart as a Parent

Mai'a Williams, author of *This Is How We Survive: Revolutionary Mothering, War, and Exile in the 21st Century*

I met Mai'a in Los Angeles around Mother's Day 2016. She was a brilliant and very matter-of-fact speaker during a panel reading and discussion on the life-affirming book *Revolutionary Mothering: Love on the Front Lines*. Making the trek from Orange County to the venue in Chinatown, I was late, so I stood in the back, smooshed between the kids' art activity table and the books for sale, in a room bursting at the seams with mothers, caregivers, and children. Mai'a shared her journey as a mother, of moving with her daughter abroad and experiencing surveillance and systemic violence. I recall nodding in agreement, as I had reflected on my own move from South Los Angeles to Orange County with my son. When it was time for the Q&A, I was nervous, but my friend, Dawn Marie, urged me to raise my hand. I shared my struggle with raising a Black boy and requested insights on how to transition from fear-based parenting to liberated parenting. That had been a question that I had been chewing on for the previous year. Mai'a's answer during that short panel left me longing for more. I followed up with her and asked if she'd be a podcast guest and the rest is history. She was my first official podcast guest. I interviewed her from my home in Orange County while she was traveling for the book tour. In our discussion, we explored segments of her writings and Mai'a shared her radical mothering principles when it comes to safety, boundaries, and resilience from trauma. Here's a snippet of what she graciously shared with me:

Breaking Apart

"While being a mother—whether it's during the pregnancy, the birth, or in taking care of the baby; or even when your kid enters elementary school years, becomes a teenager, just somewhere along that path of being a mother—you will be broken apart. For me, that's me on the floor crying—I mean like there's nothing left. I've got nothing left to give. Every mother, sooner or later, gets to that stage where it just breaks you. To me, whenever that happens, it's a bursting process. It is a moment of being traumatized. That is actually a moment in which we can make some choices. In the

"In the healing from that breaking apart and the healing from that trauma, we can choose to either become harsher, angrier, more bitter, closed off, and controlling of other people—or we can take that moment to see that, even while we are breaking apart, we haven't been broken."

—MAI'A WILLIAMS

healing from that breaking apart and the healing from that trauma, we can choose to either become harsher, angrier, more bitter, closed off, and controlling of other people—or we can take that moment to see that, even while we are breaking apart, we haven't been broken. This is actually an opportunity for me to be able to reach out and become more open, more community-oriented. It can be a pathway for us to be able to relate to our children and to other mothers, and be able to create community even more because we've had this incredibly human moment.

"This is really hard, while simultaneously being a really beautiful and amazing moment. Unfortunately, we don't get to talk about the trauma of becoming a mother, or the trauma of being a mother, very often. But that trauma can actually be the ground and the soil in which we sow very different types of seeds—for how we want to raise our children and create community."

This early conversation with Mai'a raised a couple of points for me regarding trauma. First, the idea that motherhood is traumatic—even though it's often portrayed as the most beautiful, positive, and joyful experience of a person's life. In reality, it can be completely traumatic—from infertility and challenges with conception, to complicated, near-death births, to postpartum challenges and infant phases. Secondly, Mai'a reframing trauma as soil for new seeds opened up something for me to see what's possible *because* not *in spite* of trauma. So often we talk about the need to be resilient and bounce back from trauma, but Mai'a offers what is possible in our trauma.

Liberated Parenting Strategy

Reflect

Think about a time when you felt you were "breaking apart" as a parent. As Mai'a shared, it can happen at various states of our parenting journey—from pregnancy, to birth, to elementary school, etc. As you return to that time, getting in touch with how were you feeling, think about what felt possible and impossible? What choices and options were available to you? Read Tupac Shakur's "The Rose That Grew from Concrete," a short eight-line poem about rising above one's circumstances. Using symbolism, Tupac calls our attention to a rose that does not allow dire conditions to hinder its growth; instead the rose proves nature's law is wrong. Similar to Mai'a's story, the rose in Shakur's poem leverages the cracks in the concrete to breathe fresh air. After reading the poem, reflect on a rose that has bloomed from you breaking apart.

Practice

Often, we try to present ourselves as though we "have it together" and when we experience "breaking apart," we retreat and withdraw, feeling alone and isolated.

As Mai'a shared, our moments of breaking apart are opportunities to be more expansive. Using that past experience of breaking apart to prepare for your next breakthrough, create a break-apart to breakthrough plan.

Write out: Next time you find yourself "breaking apart," consider it a moment to open up and invite your community/village into your trauma. How can you connect with your community the next time you are breaking apart?

Here are some questions to ask yourself to create a breakthrough plan:

○ When I am breaking apart it, looks, feels, sounds like:

○ When I am breaking apart, I will not judge myself, I will give myself grace and understanding by:

○ A mantra I can say to myself is:

○ A care practice I can engage in is:

○ A few people I can connect with are:

Shifting Away from Tough Love

A. Rochaun Meadows-Fernandez, writer for "On Parenting" in the *Washington Post*

On the heels of the visible upsurge of white supremacy in Charlottesville in 2017, I saw a beautiful article[1] which made the call for Black parents to spoil their children as a sort of coat or buffer of protection from the hatred being spewed. Reading the article, I had so many moments of resonance and "yessss, girl" that I decided to reach out to the author via Facebook Messenger. Here's what I sent to her:

Thank you for your much needed perspective and analysis in your recent piece in the Washington Post *about spoiling Black children! Your frame and perspective is at the core of my passion project, Parenting for Liberation. I have made a commitment to engage with folks who are raising Black children who want to shift from fear-based parenting (rooted in protection since slavery) to parenting for liberation. I would love to interview you about this piece for my podcast. I believe Black parents need to hear stories about what it means to spoil Black children given the negative connotations with spoiling (e.g., spare the rod, spoil the child). If you are interested please let's connect! For more info, www.parentingforliberation.org. Also on Facebook!*

"To be fully emotionally present for your child as a Black person is revolutionary. Truthfully it is. I don't think we have the terminology to describe free Black parents."

—A. ROCHAUN MEADOWS-FERNANDEZ

A. Rochaun responded very positively to my humble request and invited me to share my parenting reflections in her follow-up article[2] to be featured in "On Parenting" in the *Washington Post*. Following the publication, I connected with A. Rochaun for a podcast interview. We spoke by phone for the interview, and I could hear her child in the background. During our conversation, we reflected on the impact of slavery and historical traumas that lead to fear-based parenting styles such as "tough love." A. Rochaun shared how she is breaking through historical and intergenerational cycles of parenting to resist tough love.

Parenting in an Affectionate Way: Breastfeeding and Babywearing

"One of the first things that kind of sent me down the path of shifting from tough love to being fully emotionally present was deciding to breastfeed. That was the catalyst for me to acknowledge that I'm simply feeding my child in an affectionate way. I would also babywear him for ease to get things done. I was shocked by the resistance that I received from people on both sides of the fence. People would say 'Oh, don't nurse him for too long—you'll be spoiling him' or 'Don't hold that baby all the time. Then he'll be spoiled.'

"That's when I questioned: How is being emotionally present for my child spoiling him? First, taking the literal concept of *spoiling*—which is to separate and then not be any good anymore—my son is not a gallon of milk. He's not going to spoil. Then taking on the definition that they're implying—he won't be any good anymore. Again I questioned: How is being emotionally present and giving the balance of love and structure that research has already proven countless times that children excel in, spoiling him? For so long, we have been taught that to be completely present for our children is wrong."

Three Little Words: I Love You

"I grew up with a mom who obviously loves me dearly, but never felt comfortable enough to say 'I love you.' Although everything my mom does, from the way she looked to the way she smiled, just reeks love everywhere—she was never able to say those three words, because she grew up in an environment where her parents didn't tell her they loved her. Similarly, they would do their best to show it, but the words were just uncomfortable. It didn't feel right on their lips. While I love how she interacted with me and I love that she was physically present and provided me with the things I needed, I can remember how weird it felt that my mom just was never comfortable using that terminology."

Declaring Love

"Combining growing up never hearing 'I love you' from my mom with the experiences of hearing the backlash when I made the decision to breastfeed, coupled with watching all of the horrific videos of children being beaten and mistreated online—it was an accumulation of years of frustration with parenting styles. I made the choice: I'm not going to let the rest of the world dictate the amount of love I give to my child. I'm not a slave anymore, I'm claiming it for myself that I can be free. I can nurse my son because I'm not responsible for nursing someone else's child. I can be present for him because I don't have to prioritize

someone else's baby over mine. It was a personal decision and decla-
ration. I think that everyone has the ability to decide for themselves
that they're not gonna let anyone tell them how to love their kids."

My conversation with A. Rochaun was familiar and affirming—as if
talking to a cousin or sibling about our mother. Throughout our chat
about her mom's way of showing love rather than articulating it verbally,
I saw my relationship with my own mother reflected back. What was different about A. Rochaun was the amount of grace and understanding
she had for her mother. Through her own grace for her mother, a seed of
understanding was planted within me toward my mother. I want to share
a snippet from A. Rochaun's piece on Charlottesville to contextualize
her compassion and understanding of our parents' "tough love" way of
parenting and her call and imperative that our generations shift from
tough love to what I call *radical* love:

> *Our parents' method was one of sacrifice. It was a very noble goal but
> it left much to be desired. We have learned through the decades that
> we can't protect our children from the hate of the world by acclimating
> them to high levels of discipline. This is because their actions are not
> the cause for their mistreatment. We owe it to ourselves and our chil-
> dren to hold them as tight as we can. We may be the only ones to ever
> do so. It's my hope that the love I show my son will inspire a revolution.
> Black parents' capacity to love their children has been limited since
> slavery. Let's not adjust our love any longer, and maybe for the first
> generation yet, we will empower our children in ways previous gener-
> ations of black youths have never known.*

Liberated Parenting Strategy

"Had my parents been loved well by their parents they would have given that love to their children. They gave what they had been given—care. . . . But simply giving care does not mean we are loving."

—**bell hooks,** All About Love

Reflect

Spend some time reflecting on the excerpt above from *All About Love* by bell hooks. Recognizing that the word *love* can take on many different forms, reflect on your own childhood—how were you "loved"? As A. Rochaun shared, she knew her mother loved her, even though she never said those words. What did "love" look like for you as a child?

Practice

If you could offer your inner child the love that was needed, what would that look like? Take time to love on your inner child:

○ Tell her the words that she deserved to hear—maybe your inner child never heard words of affirmation like *I love you, I'm proud of you, You are beautiful.* What are the life-affirming words that you can say to your inner child?

○ Play the games your inner child yearned to play—maybe your inner child wants the freedom to play. What games and activities can you play (hopscotch, checker, cards, coloring)?

○ Offer the salve to wounds that need to be healed—maybe your inner child is hurting. What healing does she need?

Now that you have provided your own inner child love, what is possible for giving the same love to your own child(ren)?

Black Fatherhood

Neil Irvin, executive director of Men Can Stop Rape

In 2012 I was selected for the second cohort of Move to End Violence, a program that engages movement leaders working to end gender-based violence in the United States, and that's how I met Neil Irvin, who was a fellow in the first cohort. While I had heard of his incredible work as a male ally in the fight for gender equity and as executive director of Men Can Stop Rape, it wasn't until I saw him give a keynote at Black Women's Blueprint Words of Fire: Sex, Power, and a Black Feminist Call for Social Justice Conference in April 2017 that I witnessed his brilliance firsthand. I was at the conference to receive the Black Feminist Rising award and present a workshop on Parenting for Liberation. My husband accompanied me to the conference, and I was happy that he wasn't the only Black man in the room in solidarity with Black women making a call for feminism. I was surprised that a man was being given such a huge platform, but Neil showed up and cleared up any questions I had about a man's role in the feminist movement. Neil reflected on Black fatherhood, gender equity in the household, the responsibility of Black fathers keeping Black children safe, the role of Black male role models, and much more. He acknowledged how men can either be complicit in the violence or be counterparts in upending patriarchy. Following his talk, I invited him on the podcast and intentionally aired the episode on the eve of Father's Day. Here are some snippets of our conversation:

Power of Language

"Whether in school or in our home, language and communication is key to preparing our children to start their journey of learning, for the rest of their life. You are able to read a story to the child while it's still in the womb, so that it's getting used to the pattern and the tone of your voice. I experienced that reading to my children when they were in their mother's womb and when they came out at a certain point when they were more developed, I would be rereading stories that they had read when they were in their womb.

"When our children were infants, we never talked 'baby talk' to them. There's a field of research in terms of early childhood development related to infants' ability to comprehend. It's the same reason why they talk about children's ability to learn languages more easily when they're younger.

"Language is important. Communication is important. It's not only for us to be able to brag about how smart our children are, but it's for them to be able to defend themselves. We want them to be able to tell us and use the appropriate words. Our six-year-old son knows the words *penis* and *vagina* and can talk about them in developmentally appropriate ways. God forbid anything ever happens to any of our children, but we want to make sure that they know how to use the right words and communicate properly so that they're not misled or hurt.

"As parents, we were clear that we were preparing our children to be able to make sound decisions when they leave us based on critical-thinking skills. Those critical-thinking skills get shaped by gaining social-emotional intelligence—how they learn compassion, sympathy, empathy, anger, frustration. They have to know that about themselves, be able to detect those things for themselves. Then the other piece that we know is important for all people, whether children or adults, but the three things that shape personality, our nature, nurture, and environment."

Fathering Daughters

"It is important to me that my daughters know that whatever relationship they choose in their life, that relationship is going to be a reflection of what they've learned from their mother and me. I want them to know that no one will love them more than me so that they will not be manipulated, tricked, or seduced. Just because someone buys them a bouquet of flowers or a hot dog, it doesn't mean love, because they've seen what real love is. They've experienced it, been connected to it. They know how it feels. I want that for my own children, and for students we work with in the community through my organization, Men Can Stop Rape."

Modeling Healthy Masculinity

"When I work with girls through Men Can Stop Rape, I am very clear that I model the ability to have appropriate adult relationships; intergenerational relationships with adult men who can role model healthy masculinity. I want to be an example, particularly as a Black man, of how to follow our female colleagues, their leadership, respecting their guidance, their intellect, their expertise, and collaborate with one another.

"It's important for our girls to see women who are able to work with men and it not be about a romantic relationship. It's about accomplishing a task or a goal. Unfortunately, a lot of our girls learn to interact with men through sexuality—the way that they want to communicate with young men is through a flirtation. Instead, it's really important that girls are allowed to be girls and be safe enough to not have to use what we think are stereotypical kinds of characteristics to define themselves to be authorized in the space."

Black Male Accountability

"What I know is that in this country, for five hundred years, Black children have been vulnerable to a system of white supremacy that does not value them. Our children are being inundated by the media, and affected by random acts of violence, white supremacist violence, and gender-based violence. I have the most respect for adults who prioritize creating environments where young people are safe; and if you are creating an environment where young people aren't safe, you're doing harm to them and that harm ultimately spills outside of that home, into the larger community, but most importantly it impacts that child for their life. I think if our community is going to overcome some of the challenges that we're experiencing, and have historically experienced, it's going to be through our children's ability to be prepared for a global community.

"The reason many of our Black girls and boys are fleeing and running from homes is that they're being abused and neglected. That can be everything from not eating regularly to being responsible for caring for small siblings, to not getting enough expectations around school. As a result, children go looking for someone, someplace, some entity to have their needs met. We have to start being more honest about the fact that many of those reasons start with us. It's really important for Black men to be mindful of how and what space we take up in our home, how we use our authority, how we provide, how we show collaboration, how we give love and receive love. How we listen, how we act. In my opinion, Black men who are in the lives of children and adolescents, but who aren't routinely holding themselves accountable and responsible for those children's safety at all times, are doing our community a disservice. It's not about the Ku Klux Klan or neo-Nazis in the Black community. If you are an uncle, brother, father, or a neighbor—I'm all of those things—who is crossing boundaries and harming children, then you need to be rooted out of the community and held accountable. The rest of us, as a community, need to make sure that those kinds of things don't happen moving forward. I take very seriously that we create spaces and environments and families and homes where Black children are not being made vulnerable to violence that some Black men are perpetrating against them.

"We, as Black men, must always be accountable to Black girls and women and their safety, and to make sure that we're not just surviving as a community, but that we get to a place where we're thriving. The expectation is that, at all times, a Black child is most safe in the presence of Black adults."

As an adult who has worked in the gender-based violence movement for over fifteen years, I have very rarely shared that I am a survivor of child sexual abuse; however, during my conversation with Neil, my inner girl-child was seen, heard, and affirmed. Through Neil's accountability as a Black man, my childhood Black girl self who had been taken advantage of by a male family friend, feels comfort and safety.

Liberated Parenting Strategy

This conversation with Neil counteracts an ongoing myth around Black fathers as absent or inactive in their children's lives. A Center for Disease Control report[3] issued in December 2013 found that Black fathers had the most daily involvement with their children compared to any other group of fathers. Because Black fathers are engaged and active in Black children's lives, Neil is inviting us into a deeper, more intimate reflection about the role, responsibilities, and engagement of these very active Black fathers. Please note this reflection isn't limited only to fathers—anyone who has relationships and contacts with Black children can reflect on this.

During our conversation, Neil spoke on the disproportionately high number of missing Black girls in his hometown of Washington, DC, which garnered a spike in media attention in spring 2017. While there was controversy over whether the Black girls were kidnapped and trafficked or had run away, Neil's invitation here is for us to do the simultaneous reflections on the personal and political factors leading to missing Black girls—exploring both the systems outside the home while interrogating the family structure within the home.

Reflect

Neil calls for us in our multiple roles as fathers (mothers), uncles (aunties), brothers (sisters), neighbors, etc. in the lives of Black children to be accountable to ensuring Black children are safe. Reflecting on your own idea of safety: Did you feel safe as a child? Who kept you safe? How does your experience of safety impact how you see your adult role and responsibilities to keep Black children—not only our own but all Black children—safe?

Practice

Listen or watch the music video for "Runaway Love," a hip hop song by Ludacris featuring Mary J. Blige. In this song, Ludacris and Mary J. Blige tell the stories of girls between the ages of nine and ten who are living abusive, empty lives with emotionally absent and violent parents. Going through such violence in their homes, the girls are each *"trying to figure why the world is so cold . . . Forced to think that hell is a place called home."*

At the close of the song, Ludacris makes an empathetic plea to the girls:

"Close your eyes
And picture us running away together,
When we come back everything is gonna to be okay,
Open your eyes"

Reflecting on your own experiences of childhood challenges: Who were the people in your life who affirmed your experiences? What kinds of support does your inner child now need to hear from you? Remind your inner child that you are safe.

Finding a Village: How to Build a Black Community

Malesha Taylor, classically trained opera singer; founder of museSalon Collaborative

As I was building up Parenting for Liberation, I was searching for conferences and learning opportunities to nurture this idea I had given birth to. In fall 2017 I attended the Brioxy Summit in Los Angeles, where attendees were invited to develop our skills as leaders, strategize around the work we were building, and deepen our toolkit in self-care. It was there that I met so many amazing leaders, artists, and entrepreneurs of color—one of whom was Malesha Taylor, a classically trained opera singer and mother of three, residing in San Diego, a suburban community in Southern California. At the summit, we swapped business cards to discuss collaborating and supporting one another as mothers of color parenting in suburbia. During our discussion, Malesha reflected on the trauma of her own childhood, growing up in California's suburbs as the only Black kid. She shares tips on how to manifest and build community in spaces that feel isolating, through the use of arts and culture. With a commitment to "never be the only," Malesha advocates for centering Black voices and other marginalized communities in the arts, through her organization, museSalon Collaborative and through her work as a vanguard Black opera singer. Here's an excerpt of our conversation:

Growing Up "Different"

"I grew up in Los Angeles County, in the suburbs. I didn't really have an idea of a Black community here, other than the Black church. I didn't really have a sense of culture or Black Liberation.

"When I was growing up, I was almost always the only Black person in every environment (except when I was with family). However, my family didn't go out of their way to make sure I had Black friends, so I felt a lot of discomfort, including psychological discomfort. When I reflect on it, I always knew that I was different.

"It didn't help that I had to explain myself everywhere I went. From questions about my hair ('Oh Malesha, you have braids and your hair is long this week, but last week you had a ponytail. What's up with that?') to dating (when it was time for a school dance, I had to hope some white guy was going to invite me). As a young girl, I often felt kind of different and undesirable. Now, as a parent, I think it's important that my kids have some relief and not have to experience that all the time. I am creating spaces for them where they are bonding and building relationships with other Black kids and other Black leaders, elders, aunties, and uncles. We are building and filling that village so that they always have a village to identify with and to fall back on."

Finding Home in a Different World

"As a young adult, when I lived in Brooklyn, I got to a place where I could wear my natural hair and explore all of its different shapes. It's a fuller diaspora of Black people there—there's African, Caribbean, the migration of Black people from the South. I really got to see the beauty of our people there—from owning our own businesses to talking to each other and being happy to see each other in the neighborhood. While leasing, all of my landlords were Black so I got to see Black people owning property and I paid rent to people that looked like me. While walking down the street, I saw people who knew my name—this was just totally different from how I grew up.

"Now I live in San Diego, California. Moving here from Brooklyn was a really life-changing experience which helped in further developing my identity as a Black woman. In San Diego, there's 8 percent Black people, which is small but substantial, because it means that the Black people here know each other. Since we're such a small community, we are able to build deep bonds and connections. I've recently discovered other families that share similar values and I make time to hang out with them. I've identified individuals like these and slowly created a village. There are at least ten folks that I celebrate Kwanzaa with every year who I can call for babysitting, host a book club with, and just create a network."

Another White World

"I sing at the opera, which is a similar phenomenon to my childhood because it's a very white space for me as well, although I am working on decolonizing the arts. I've been in the theater opera world since high school, and back then I knew I was the only Black kid and I knew that it was a predominantly white space, but it wasn't deeply affecting me because my whole day was that way. I always tried to blend in; I wasn't trying to stick out, so my Blackness was very subdued. However, now that I've lived in Brooklyn and experienced a real Black village, my Blackness is a part of what keeps me stable and whole. Now, I'm working with Art for a Changing America and some other campaigns on decolonizing the arts and pushing for racial justice and representation in the arts. I formed my collaborative, museSalon, to be a resource to other artists like myself to be able to financially sustain themselves."

Malesha's story is so real and relatable to me. While I grew up sharing my time between my home in Watts and my grandparents' house in Compton, I found myself the only Black girl in elementary school but surrounded by Latinx kids. I remember not knowing the dominant language and feeling left out. I know the difference my son is feeling now, being raised in Orange County as one of the very few Black kids in predominantly white schools. I work really hard and intentionally to surround him with Blackness when he is outside of school and on weekends. I know that every bit helps to instill pride and sense of self.

Liberated Parenting Strategy

Reflect

Growing up in isolation and disconnected from a village can have impacts on sense of self, such as the discomfort Malesha described. Reflecting on your own lived experiences in the United States, where African Americans make up only 13 percent of the population, have you had experiences of being isolated or the "only"? What was the impact of being "alone"?

Explore

Often, when we are the "only," a strategy for safety is to blend in and not stand out. This diminishing of self, identity, and culture can have traumatic impacts on self-identity. Explore ways that you can maintain identity and cultural pride even when isolated. While Malesha had the experience of visiting a culturally diverse space such as Brooklyn, how can you connect to culture where you are? Research and explore the local cultural centers and museums in your area.

Practice

To counter the narratives of othering, listen to "I Love Being Black" by activist group BYP100 and write down five things you love about your Blackness. Take those five things and create your own affirmation statement called "I Love Being Black." Incorporate this affirmation into your daily routine (e.g., a post-it on your bathroom mirror to recite). I recommend reciting it to yourself at least three times a day. Spend time affirming your Blackness, allowing it to fill you up from the inside out.

Watering Your Creativity

Jena Holliday, creator of #100DaysofMotherhoodSOF; owner and illustrator of Spoonful of Faith design studio

My good friend Scheherazade Tillet always sends me links to support my work, and because she's also an artist, she sent me an *Essence* series called "Black Girls Draw," featuring Jena Holliday, who was quoted saying, "One of the greatest revolutionary acts as a Black person in America is Black motherhood."[4] I couldn't agree more! Coupled with such powerful words were beautiful illustrations of Black motherhood (the beautiful and hard moments, from when mothers are breaking apart to moments when they are holding it all down beautifully). I was blown away by Jena's commitment to depicting Black mothers while also being a mother herself. So I reached out to Jena first to thank her for her commitment to me/her/us, and then to commission a piece of my son and me, and invite her to be a guest on the podcast. She revealed her amazing artist rendition of me and my son during our recorded phone call. After I fanned out over the way she captured the essence of my mommy-son relationship, we discussed her 100 Days of Motherhood campaign that represents the power of Black motherhood. In our discussion, Jena shared why she wanted to focus on Black motherhood, the importance of representation in art, and how being a mother inspired her own creativity. Here are some highlights from our conversation:

Creativity as Resourcefulness

"I grew up in a large family. I'm one of seven kids. I've been super creative since I was young. My parents, while they took great care of us, did not have everything to give us all the time, which made me and my siblings super creative with what we had. For example, I learned HTML and coding in middle school because I wanted a cute website and I couldn't afford to pay for it. It's always been inside of me, to be creative. However, as I advanced in school, I started to listen to my teachers or other people saying that a path following art and creativity wasn't going to get me money. Instead of going toward arts, I actually ended up going to school for marketing and business.

"About four years ago, I rediscovered my faith and really felt this strong pull inside of me to do all of those creative things that I had done as a child. Around the same time, I became pregnant with my first child, and becoming a mother really pushed me even further back into my creativity. I started thinking about living in my truth. How can I tell my daughter she can be anything that she can dream, or tell her to go after the things that are inside of her heart, if I am not doing it myself? I would say that my faith and motherhood were truly my inspiration to get me started back on that path."

Shining a Light

"As an illustrator, I know many great artists and illustrators in the industry. However, people of color artists and illustrators are not being highlighted as much, and as a result, we as people of color are not being featured as illustrations. When I add the layer of me being a Black woman and a mother, I feel even more overlooked. I have decided to use my illustrations as a way for me to shine a light on Black women who are on the ride of motherhood. There's something really special about motherhood, so I highlight mothers simply doing what they were called to do—to raise children in this day and age as Black women."

Seeing the Beauty in the Everyday

"For my project, 100 Days of Motherhood SOF (Spoonful of Faith), I pick Black mothers that inspire me online and draw illustrations of them reflecting everyday moments of Black motherhood. After illustrating, I'd share publicly on Instagram using the hashtag #100DaysofMotherhoodSOF, and each time I shared an illustration of a Black mom, it was like fireworks—not only in the Black community but in diverse communities everywhere. Because Black women aren't seen, there was a resounding affirmation to lift up and be in community with Black woman. I'm just shining a light. The project goal is to illustrate one hundred moms, and I'm about halfway through. What I really loved was being able to empower women and kind of secretly do that. The moms selected don't know that they are going to be featured. The excitement of them discovering themselves and that someone saw them in their fullness and thought that the work they were doing as mothers—the everyday—was good enough to share and shine a light on it.

"A really great part of the project is showing that there's beauty in hard and painful moments. I know as moms sometimes we don't see it that way, but we should. In photos online, I witnessed that so many moms don't even show their faces, they just show their kids. In the illustrations, I show the moms to remind them they're a part of this too. It makes my heart swell to, like, give the illustration to someone, so they can see themselves, their beauty and power in the everyday."

Watering Your Creativity

"Last year, I felt the need to create a space called Mother Creative, a space where we as women and mothers can come together and empower each other. In the space, I share tools and experiences that I've had using creativity. My desire is for people to go after their God-given dreams and become everything they're created to be. Unfortunately, when people become mothers, there's a lot of things that shift. For some, there's a conception and birth that propels them forward; but for others, it makes them feel really stuck and they are unsure how to chase

> **"Sometimes motherhood is going to be really tough and you're not going to feel like you have time for creativity, but if you continue to water it, it can grow into something even greater."**
>
> **—JENA HOLLIDAY**

after the things that they've desired or dreamed. Some get stuck in the belief that 'Oh, I'm just supposed to mother,' while others don't know how to juggle and balance it all. I took an initiative to create a space that doesn't exist to challenge moms to get creative in their life as it is today, right now. During each gathering, I walk the moms I work with through each season, explaining that every season is not going to be the same. Sometimes motherhood is going to be really tough and you're not going to feel like you have time for creativity, but if you continue to water it, it can grow into something even greater."

Jena's story beautifully weaves together mothering and creativity in that she uses her creativity to reveal the messy and challenging parts of parenting, as well as to help get her through those hard times. Unfortunately, when things get messy, challenging, and busy, we cut the things that feel "extra," which often means eliminating things that bring us joy, like playing, reading a good book, rest, and our creativity. In a society centered on our productivity, when we feel forced to choose between using thirty minutes of "downtime" (I put that in quotes because those of us with kids know that there is really no such thing) to do that load of laundry, or to take a nap or listen to a podcast (Parenting for Liberation episode, anyone?), many of us would opt to get "the thing" done or, attempting to be superhuman multitaskers, we'd try to do both (i.e., listen to a podcast while doing the laundry). However, as Jena's story reflects so well, we must make a commitment to ourselves to create space for our creativity and to not see time coloring, painting, playing, or resting as unproductive. When we water our own creativity, we have more resources, energy, and presence for our children. This idea of watering our creativity really resonates with me, as it reminds me of the saying "You can't pour from an empty cup." How are we to support and nurture our own children's creativity, ingenuity, and innovation when we don't water our own?

Need more convincing? There is data within the art therapy community that shows the benefits of art as a healing medium. According to Cathy Malchiodi's article "Drawing a Picture of Health: An Art Therapy Guide," "Creative expression has been shown to naturally calm the body. Opening up through artistic expression can improve one's outlook and communicate our experiences of illness, trauma, grief, and loss."[5]

Liberated Parenting Strategy

Reflect

Jena invites us to reconnect to our childhood dreams using art and creativity. Using an art form of your preference (options below), reflect on the dreams you had as a child: How can you tap into your dreams and creativity?

In her Mother Creative space, Jena encourages parents to reclaim their dreams and aspirations through creativity as adults. Rather than seeing parenting as a hindrance, Jena uses parenthood as a catalyst to fulfilling her dreams. Using an art form of your choosing, reflect on any dreams you may have let go of or put on pause since becoming a parent.

Practice

Let's unleash our inner artists! Now I know what some of you are thinking—*I am not artistic! I can't even draw a straight line!*—and I can relate. First, art goes beyond writing tools and paper; and second, art expression is less about the product that you create and more about the process of expressing yourselves in a new medium. Here are some art forms that you can explore as you reconnect to self:

○ Make some noise: Listen to music, write your own lyrics, sing, or play an instrument.
○ Get moving and grooving: Move your body as self-expression; that can be dance, stretch, yoga, or miming.
○ Paint the town: Pick up your favorite tool whether it be paint, acrylics, markers, crayons, oil pastels, or chalk pastels.
○ Be-You-Tiful: Do makeup, paint faces, or design tattoos.
○ Get crafty: Collage, sew, or knit.
○ Say cheese: Grab a camera—it can be even your cell phone (selfie, anyone?)—pick your favorite muse, and start snapping.
○ Lights, camera, action: Similar to photography, but with motion and sound! Grab a camera and begin recording.

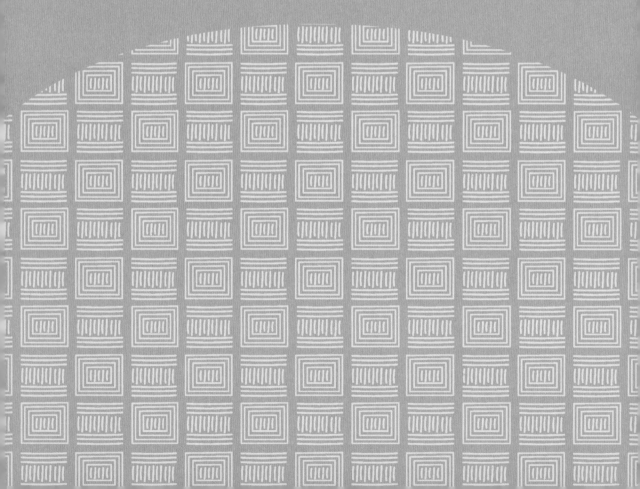

SECTION 2

(Re)connection to Our Children

SECTION 2

(Re)connection to Our Children

Section Two focuses on (re)connection to our children. Now that we have had time to reflect on our own personal experiences as children, we are better positioned to relate to our own children from a place of understanding. Exploring our own life experiences will help us to become more aware of the impact of these experiences on how we parent, and get more in tune with our childhood experiences, which helps us make meaningful connections with our current children. This is the second step on the path to parenting for liberation: to show up in right relationship with our children by holding their humanity, feelings, and experiences at the center of parenting.

Throughout this section are stories from Black parents who are shifting their parenting techniques to (re)connect with their child(ren). These shifts include creating mutual and equitable relationships with our children that honor their identity and truths; engaging in family practices that integrate children's voices; and choosing environments that help elevate our children's sense of ethnic and cultural pride.

This section is broken into subsections with multiple stories from parents in several areas of high importance for Black families: Communication and Agreements, as well as Conversations about Sex and Consent, History and Oppression, and Police Violence. Following the stories of (re)connection to our children are invitations to explore new ways to practice (re)connecting with our children through various liberated parenting strategy exercises. The exercises engage a variety of reflection approaches such as poetry, music, videos, journaling, and art. We want to invite multiple ways of learning. Our hope is that these stories offer opportunities to try on ways of being, conversation starters, and strategies to test with our children in our journey toward (re)connection.

Family Practices: Open Communication and Family Agreements

I n the following two stories, Mai'a Williams and I share how we connect with our children in our daily ways of being: from the ways we speak and communicate safely and openly with our children, to the ways we create structure in the home. Upholding the values that inform our work as activists fighting for justice, both of us as Black mothers intentionally integrate our practices of equity and mutuality in our relationship with their children—which is foundational to operationalizing liberation in our homes. Mai'a shared:

Open Communication

"The most important thing to me is that my daughter and I have very close, intimate communication. I have worked very hard to unlearn some of the things I've learned from my parents and my grandparents, and to make sure that my daughter knows that I am the safe harbor—that she can come to me no matter what. I know I am raising a person who the rest of the world may not want to exist—so I tell my daughter that, while the world out there might be difficult, strange, and sometimes weird to navigate, I will always have your back 110 percent. I know there has to be one person in my daughter's life who has her back—and that's me.

"If I say 'You can tell me anything,' I have to be the person who can accept her telling me anything. I can't create the kind of relationship where she doesn't want to tell me things because she thinks I might get upset or she might get in trouble.

"I definitely grew up with more traditional Black parents. I was afraid to tell my mother and grandmother things because I would get in trouble or they'd get upset. As a child, I decided it was better if I worked some things out on my own; but now when I look back, I do wish that there were things that I could've felt comfortable going to my mother with. I wish I knew that she was going to take it in the spirit of openness and listening, rather than responding with criticism and judgment. I work really hard to unlearn those patterns and to really dig down and listen every day, all the time. So that when something does happen to my daughter—and it has, there's been times for example, when people said really questionable things to her—she comes to me, and I've been really happy that she told me about them. Open communication is something that's very important because it means our children aren't going to be afraid of getting in trouble."

Liberated Parenting Strategy

Reflect

We often tell our children, "You can tell me anything." Think back to a time your child(ren) told you something difficult to hear. How did you respond? What worked/didn't work about the conversation? How did you show up in the conversation? Were you open? Did emotions rise—how did you respond to emotions? Who directed the conversation? Did you give your opinion?

While that reflection may have given rise to ideas on how you could have done things differently in that situation, there is no one right way to have a conversation.

Practice

Below is an offering I created through my practice as a parent and as I am developing strategies and tools for Parenting for Liberation about ways to engage in O.P.E.N. conversations with Black children. These strategies are a way of being that centers liberation of both the parent and child(ren) in dialogue.

Parenting for Liberation's O.P.E.N. Parenting Practice

O—OPEN AND OBSERVANT

Psychologists attest to the fact that parenting while Black causes levels of stress. Data shows that stress caused by social injustice has an impact on how people think.[6] All of that stress can take up valuable mind space and leave our thoughts cluttered and unclear. It's important to create open space for your child to share and talk with you. That means being present to your child. Give your child(ren) attention by removing or turning off any distractions (both external and internal noise). We understand that it can be hard sometimes, so be honest with yourself and your child if you can't be present in that moment. Let your child know another time that they can have your full attention. During the conversation, be observant of your child's cues. Let them take the lead. Don't push the conversation.

When my son Terrence was about two years old and I was on my laptop while at home, he would close the laptop on my hands when he wanted my attention. At that age he couldn't verbalize that he wanted my attention. It was an opportunity to notice and be observant of his needs. Now as a ten-year-old, Terrence calls my name over and over—"Mom, Mom, Mom" (kind of like Stewie from *Family Guy*)—and he will wait until I verbally acknowledge him before he asks me a question.

Notice the cues that your child may want your attention—Are they crying? Calling your name? Clingy? How do you know when they want your attention, and how do you respond?

Examples:

○ "Aw sweetie, I notice you are crying, what do you need? A hug? To talk? How can Mommy/Daddy help?"

○ "Hey baby, I just got home from work/school/grocery shopping and I need a few minutes to settle in, is that okay?"

P—PRAISE

In Dr. Joy DeGruy's work on post-traumatic slave syndrome, she shares a story of a maladaptive behavior of enslaved parents who belittle their children to keep them out of the eyes of the slave master. The habits have been passed on for generations and now many Black parents denigrate their children to protect them. In a world that tells us and our children that we aren't enough or our lives are disposable, it's important that we as parents praise our children and lift them up. When you're talking with your child(ren), celebrate and acknowledge them for sharing how they feel. Acknowledge their vulnerability. Praise their effort and strength for opening up. This will encourage them to share more with you in the future.

Examples:

○ "Baby girl, I know this might be scary to talk about, so I am so proud of you for sharing with me."

○ "Wow, you are so caring and have such a huge heart."

E—EMOTIONS AND EMPATHY

Too often, Black boys are told that crying and having feelings are signs of weakness; and on the other hand, Black girls who express themselves are labeled the "angry Black girl" and told to tone it down. While the world can't handle our children's emotions, it's important that in our homes we create space for our children to express how they feel. Remember that emotions are okay. Empathize with your child(ren). Validate their feelings; don't downplay them.

Examples:

○ "Son, it's okay to cry. Crying is a natural response to sadness. Don't be ashamed to cry. Daddy/Mommy cries too."

○ "You know I was once told that crying was like taking your soul to the laundromat (which basically means it's like cleaning your soul, mind)."

○ "I notice you are angry/upset and that's okay. We get upset when we are hurt. Do you want to tell me why you are upset?"

N—NONJUDGMENTAL AND NONDIRECTIONAL

Black parents are often hypervigilant, always worrying if their child(ren) will become the next victim. Because of this constant fear of threat, we want our children to be perfect, to make the right moves, because one minor wrong turn could cost their life—so we are often on alert, ready to solve a problem. While we know the stakes are high for Black babies, being a reactionary parent doesn't help. We need to create a nonjudgmental space for our children to tell us their truths (and mistakes). Listen without judgment and without giving directions. Sometimes all our children want is to be heard, and not to hear what you think they should do. Try not to impose your own solutions on your child. Help your child to figure out what they need.

Examples:

○ "It's okay to tell me what's wrong, and I promise I won't get mad or upset with you."

○ "I hear that you are upset/sad/frustrated/embarrassed/happy/ excited because of [repeat back what your child shared]."

○ "I am so sorry/happy that happened. What do you think you want to do?"

○ "How do you want me to help?"

Follow-up Reflection

Reflecting on Parenting for Liberation's O.P.E.N. strategies, what resonates for you? What feels hard for you? Which of these practices do you already engage in? Which of these practices feel challenging? Reflect on the previous conversation you had with your child(ren). What would be different if you used this O.P.E.N. approach?

Shifting from Rules to Agreements

After recording my first few episodes, I had gotten comfortable being on the asking side of the interview, so I was nervous when I was invited on *The D Report* podcast with Daniel Diaz to discuss Parenting for Liberation. My nerves shot through the roof when I learned that the podcast not only aired online but also on KUCR 88.3 FM. I'll let you all in on a little secret . . . come closer, so no one else hears this . . . I'm not particularly fond of the sound of my own voice. I know you're probably asking, Well, why did you start a podcast? As I shared briefly in the intro, I was learning so much from Black parents, that I thought it would be selfish to not share with other Black parents. I began recording these conversations assuming that my own airtime would be minimal—I would be asking questions and listening, but that's not how it works. By inviting folks into conversations to share about their parenting journeys, I also had to open up and share with them—in mutuality. So here I am with this conundrum of trying to limit how much I have to hear myself speak when I am asked to be the interviewee. Well, I pushed past my fears, and accepted the interview—twice! Daniel and I spoke in mid-2016, and again in 2017. Here is a snippet of what I shared with Daniel during my first interview:

"I've been reading various books about new ways to be in relationships with young people. The book is called *All About Love: New Visions* by bell hooks. There's a chapter in the book called 'Justice: Childhood Love Lessons.' I'll read a passage:

> *Loving parents work hard to discipline without punishment. They focus on teaching children how to be self-disciplining and how to take responsibility for their own actions.*

"One way I'm trying this practice is I shifted from having house 'rules' to house 'agreements.' In setting the agreements, we discussed what I needed from my son, Terrence, and he shared what he needed from me to support him. Instead of just 'Listen to me because I say so,' I shared why I need him to listen to me. Then he requested that I not get 'frustrated' and raise my voice. We both agreed that was more mutual. I'm sure it probably sounds weird to parents because I was raised by traditional Black folks who say: 'It's my house and my rules. Until you're eighteen, you have to listen to me.' But there's something more powerful when young people feel like they have a sense of agency. Then they're not just listening to the rules, they actually have something to contribute. They feel more committed because it's an agreement and they have responsibilities too."

Liberated Parenting Strategy

Reflect

In my story, I suggest shifting from "house rules" to "house agreements" with your children. Not only do adults have specific requests and needs but children also need specific support from us as parents. Spend some time with your child(ren) to reflect on what their individual needs are. Sit together and create a list of agreements that both parties can commit to. Ask your child to come up with solutions that are fair, safe, aligned with your family's values, and mutually agreeable. Remember that each child-parent relationship is unique, so separate agreements may be needed for each child.

Practice

I recommend making O.P.E.N. one of your first family agreements. Share O.P.E.N. with your child(ren) and get their feedback. Maybe they can partner with you in making sure that each of you is practicing. Next time you're having a conversation, you can check with one another: "Are you being O.P.E.N.?" or "Are you O.P.E.N. to talk to me right now?"

During my family agreements conversation with Terrence, it became clear to me that my response in moments of conflict were visibly frustrated. Thus, my commitment was to check myself. I'm not perfect, and use the following process to *acknowledge, account,* and *adapt* from frustration:

Parenting for Liberation's AAA for Frustration

Acknowledge: "Hold on, I notice I'm getting frustrated," or "Oh, shoot! I just raised my voice at you and that's not how you deserve to be spoken to and that's not how I want to speak to you."

Account: "I'm sorry for yelling/raising my voice/being frustrated. I want to account/apologize for my behavior and the impact it is having on you. Do you want to tell me how it made you feel?" Listen to the impact you had, then account for it—"I apologize that my yelling made you scared, worried, etc."

Adapt: "In the future, instead of yelling, I will pause and breathe when I feel myself getting frustrated. It would be really helpful if you can help me by pointing out if you notice me getting frustrated."

Conversations about Sex(uality) and Consent

Ignacio Rivera, founder/director of The HEAL Project

Talking about sex in a liberated way is a challenge. Oftentimes, we have conversations about sex rooted in fear—fear of unintended pregnancy, fear of sexually transmitted infections, fear of sexual abuse and violence, etc. Because it is so scary, many parents avoid it. Simply because you don't talk about sex with your child, doesn't mean your child is not learning about it elsewhere. I learned that the hard way, when I was discussing sexism with my then third grader and he chuckled whenever I said "sexism." I asked him what was so funny. He said, "Mom, you keep saying SEX-ism." I got curious and asked him why the word *sex* made him laugh but before he could answer, I blurted out, "Do you know what sex is?" in shock and lack of readiness to have this conversation. He responded that his friend in third grade told him. Nervously, I asked what this third grader had told him, and he described it to me as parents lying in bed in their underwear and kissing. While I knew there was more I could explain, I left the third-grade explanation and exited that conversation quickly by returning to the conversation about sexism (which, to be honest, is just as complex to explain to a third grader, but one I was more comfortable having. To learn how to have those types of conversations, read on for my conversation with Tiffany Lanoix, which is next in this section). After stumbling through that conversation, I knew I needed support. A member of my beloved community, Emanuel Brown, who is an incredible connector of people, ideas, and visions, linked me with Ignacio Rivera, who created the groundbreaking, heartfelt, and witty online talk show *Pure Love* with their daughter Amanda to discuss talking with kids about sexuality. I shared this incident with Ignacio and Amanda, and they offered practical ideas for how to have conversations with our children about sex(uality) and other related topics, such as sexual health and consent. Here is a snippet of the wisdom that Ignacio and Amanda shared with me:

Normalizing the Conversation

"A lot of people get really hard on themselves when they don't have conversations with their kids about sex. Or they say they didn't do it right, but really, everybody does it in their own way. What I'm trying to push is that we actually have the conversations—no matter if we fumble or if we don't know all of the answers—just make it normal. When parenting for liberation, you want to raise your child in a way that eliminates the fear in regard to race and class, but it's also the same around sex and sexuality. Not talking about sex and sexuality is completely fear-based. Everything about sex is made to be scary—and yes, there's some scary things—but there are some beautiful and wonderful things there too that we should know about."

MORE THAN ONCE

"I suggest bringing sex up—but not as just a one-time conversation because that adds a lot of pressure to the both of you. This conversation is more than once. It's all the time in different aspects—for example, you can talk about relationships or actual sex or masturbation or sexual violence."

ICEBREAKER

"One way to bring it up is through an icebreaker—for example, you and your child might see a movie or something on social media that could spark a dialogue. Even while asking about their day, you may find an opening for a conversation."

ASK/TELL ME ANYTHING DAY

"Another way to bring it up is by having recurring 'no repercussions' conversations [which can also be reframed as 'ask/tell me anything' conversations, depending on your comfort level]. This is a day that we would go to a café and sit and get tea and snacks. You can actually pick the category, *Jeopardy*-style, like sex, race, class, etc. Ask your child: *What category do you want to talk about? We can talk about anything at all and you can't get in trouble*. This became an opportunity for my child to ask me or tell me anything she wanted to, including confessions, and she would not have any repercussions for that. It was also an opportunity for me to ask follow-up questions and we could go back and forth, and discuss.

"One thing with young people is that a lot of times they're scared—totally terrified, even—to bring something up. The 'no repercussions' strategy worked really nicely because she would say things that she probably would have never brought up otherwise. It's actually showing them that they can trust you. You can set up the parameters the way you would like—you and your child(ren) could come up with those parameters together. This also shows good boundary-setting and negotiation skills."

NOT ON THE KID

"Lastly, you can also let them know that if they want to talk to you about anything, you're there. However, I would caution against putting all your eggs in that basket because it's putting the burden on children to have the courage to come to you and say something—something that you are struggling to say to them yourself. While it's okay to say that, don't rely on it completely because as guardians and parents, it is our job to have the conversation. We have to push through the silence—even when they say, 'Leave me the hell alone,' we have to continue to approach the conversation."

Sex Education Is More Than Sex—Conversations about Consent

"Sex education is also about how kids form friendships, how children are able to create their own boundaries, and are able to say, 'No, I don't like that' or 'I would like to do this.' That's building the blocks for consent in the that they have a strong understanding of their own personal space—which is part of sex education.

"I work with children and I try to find little ways to teach them about consent because we are a society where the rape culture is ridiculous. One way that I teach them about consent is when one kid gets upset because another kid is not sharing their toy. I approach the kid who's upset and ask, 'What's going on? Why are you crying?' The kid says, 'Well, she didn't want to give me her toy,' and I tell the kid that that's okay because it's her toy and she has the choice whether to say yes or no. I tell the kid that they can ask her about the toy and when she gives you an answer you may not like that answer but you can't do anything about that because that belongs to her. I reinforce that it's her choice to make. Interactions like that may seem small and they may not realize it now, but later when another situation arises, they'll think before they act on something. It's important that she uses her voice to make choices about her toys and what belongs to her because, unfortunately, in that scenario, some adults may tell the little girl to 'share and be nice.' But this teaches children to trust their gut, so when something feels wrong they have that gut instinct. Unfortunately they don't trust their gut a lot of the times because it's not backed up by information, or it's catapulted by fear."

Modeling Conversations: Sex Education by Proxy

"Many people say, 'I'm so nervous about talking about sex,' or 'Sometimes my child doesn't want to talk about sex or their bodies.' One strategy that I used with my child Mandy was what I call *sex education by proxy*. What do I mean by that? You know how when you hang out at the house and you're talking with your friends, and your kids are hanging around and they're listening? This is an opportunity to have a sex-education conversation by proxy, where you would have a conversation with your friend about a sex-related topic—anything that you think that talking to them directly about would make them feel embarrassed. This allows you to [model having sexual-health conversations comfortably] and give your point of view, so your kids have the opportunity to listen and learn from you, even if you're not really talking to them directly."

> "We don't want to share, but sharing often humanizes us and makes us vulnerable. We have to make ourseves vulnerable. If we want our kids to open up . . . then we have to give a little too."
> —IGNACIO RIVERA

Being Vulnerable

"We have power over our children, and a lot of parents don't talk about things because it gives our children leverage. We don't want to share, but sharing often humanizes us and makes us vulnerable. We have to make ourselves vulnerable. If we want our kids to open up and talk to us about the thing that they're going to do for the first time—such as the first kiss or sex, or about pregnancy and STI prevention, healthy relationships, or sexuality—then we have to give a little too."

Resources and Tips

Talk with Your Kids has helpful timelines and tips developed by Planned Parenthood Los Angeles and Essential Access Health to help you build mutual trust and respect with your child(ren) and have developmentally appropriate conversations about their bodies, consent, and sexual health.

Since this conversation with Ignacio and Amanda, I have revisited the conversation with my kids about sex. We talk about this matter-of-factly rather than having a "serious talk." While he still has nervous giggles when Mom talks about sex, he knows that I am comfortable with any of his questions. When my answers are too much, he tells me, "Okay, Mom, too much." I purchased him the book *Sex Is a Funny Word* by Cory Silverberg and Fiona Smyth, which was recommended by Ignacio and Amanda. While he didn't want me to read it with him, he did take it up to his room, and he knows he can ask me any questions. Beyond my children understanding the specifics of the act of sex, what I took away as critical from my discussion with Ignacio and Amanda was for my children to practice consent (asking for and demanding) and boundaries (respecting others' boundaries and setting their own). We have since discussed consent and boundaries using what-if scenarios not exclusive to sex-related topics.

Liberated Parenting Strategy

Reflect

Take a look at Ignacio Rivera's Sexuality Talk Tips, as presented in "The Evolution of the Talk" in Thrive: A Year of Skill-Shares by and for People Impacted by Domestic and Sexual Violence series organized by Gather Together:

1. Avoid announcing that you are about to have "the talk." The talk is never one conversation, but many.
2. Talk with your children. Avoid talking at your children from a top-down perspective.
3. Talk about sexuality as often as you can. Use media—movies, music, books, and social media—to talk with them about sex.
4. Ask them questions!
5. Share stories and humanize yourself.
6. Never shame, use fear tactics, or shut down a conversation about sex, no matter how uncomfortable you feel.
7. Never yuck anyone's yum—don't speak ill about sexual practices or sexual orientation.

8. Teach from many perspectives, so your child learns to have a critical mind on sex.
9. If you don't know information about a particular topic, research it together or look it up and share the information with your child(ren).
10. Talk about sex matter-of-factly. Remember, this is natural.

Steps to Sexuality Talks with Your Child(ren)

1. Our bodies, consent, and boundary setting—Teach your children the proper names for their body parts. Make it fun. Do regular boundary and consent exercises with them, and model behavior.
2. Communication by proxy—Discuss love, dating, rape culture, homophobia, sexism, and lots more, by proxy. Have a deep conversation with your friend in front of your children. Your children are always listening so make sure to talk from different perspectives and state the issue clearly.
3. Teachable media—Have a movie night with your child and afterward get dessert and talk it over. Ask questions and engage. Every movie has a teachable moment about friendship, love, sex, or violence.

STORY 9

Conversations about History and Oppression

Tiffany Lanoix, associate professor of sociology
at West Los Angeles College

Tiffany Lanoix has been in my sister-mama village since we met in a prenatal yoga class as first-time mamas-to-be. I was drawn to Tiffany in that class. Maybe it was her deep breathing, or maybe it was her radiating energy, or maybe it was because she was one of the few other Black women in the class. Whatever it was, we connected and have been friends ever since. It's been a beautiful, evolving sisterhood-motherhood, from prenatal yoga to mommy-and-me yoga, then mommy-and-me swim, basketball teams, birthday parties, and more. She is definitely a sister-mama in my village of support. Connecting as mamas of Black boys, we engage in all types of conversations about mothering and justice, and did I mention that Tiffany is a brilliant sociology professor? When I needed support on how to have conversations with my kids about oppressions—racism, sexism, classism, heterosexism—she answered the call. Similar to the talk about sex, to raise liberated kids, we must educate them on inequities that they may face. Below is Tiffany Lanoix on how she regularly looks for opportunities to discuss isms with her son:

Everyday Conversations

"I really try to create a relationship and atmosphere with my son where we are constantly talking about inequality, racism, sexism, homophobia—all of these issues and topics. When Thanksgiving comes, we talk about it specifically, but I also try to have these kinds of conversations all the time and I really try to make them low pressure. I don't say, 'Sit down, son, I am now going to tell you about sexism or about racism.' Instead, I look for everyday opportunities to bring it up."

Discussing Colonization Over Lunch

"Once I was at a restaurant with my son and I noticed there was a huge mural on the wall depicting the history of the colonization of Latin America. I took that as an opportunity to start a conversation with him. Rather than leading the discussion, I asked, 'Do you see what they're portraying?' and we talked about what was being depicted on the mural—essentially Europeans with guns holding Indigenous people hostage. We then made the connections to how that history fits into how America became the United States and what's happening currently.

"For me, it's really important to simply look for those opportunities to have these kinds of conversations in a very casual, everyday way. So that by the time Thanksgiving comes, he's ready for it, he's primed for it. It's not going to slap him upside the head and be something that he's never thought about before. He's able to place it into a larger context of race relations, racism, etc. That's an important element for me: making sure that it's a low-pressure thing and that it's a constant conversation."

Discussing Classism in the Car

"Just yesterday we were leaving my mom's house (she lives in Ingle-wood, a predominantly Black area in Los Angeles), and he asked, 'Mom, why is it that there's so many Black people that live over here, but where we live, there's not as many?' That opened up a conversation about race, class, opportunity, and how the amount of money you make determines where you live.

"Another time, he was noticing the area that my dad lives in has a lot of trash on the ground and he reflected, 'Where we live, there's not a lot of trash.' We live in Culver City, a middle-class neighborhood in Los Angeles, and my dad lives in a low-income neighborhood. I responded, 'The city is supposed to keep public areas clean; it is part of a city's social services. Where we live, there's more money for the city to do things like that. Where Papa lives, there's not as much money. So, those kinds of social services don't necessarily happen as often or to the same quality as they do in our neighborhood.'"

Discussing Generational Wealth Gaps Over Dinner

"Eventually, we actually started talking about how racism can be perpetuated from one generation to another. He knows that we've been saving to buy a house, and he had another white friend whose parents were also saving to buy a house. They were able to purchase their home, while we were still saving. They told me that part of how they were able to do it was that their parents gave them money to help with the down payment. We were talking about that and I said to him, 'Mommy and Daddy's parents didn't have as much opportunity to get an education so they couldn't get good-paying jobs that would allow them to build up money and pass that on to us.'

"I said, 'Mommy and Daddy have to basically come up with it ourselves, but your friend's grandparents were able to give them money because they had opportunities to get more education and to get good jobs and were able to pass that on. So, can you see how racism can actually be passed from one generation to the next?' And he said, 'Yeah.' Maybe he did see it, maybe he didn't; but if you keep having those little conversations, even if they don't get it all the way the first time you say it, it'll start processing, little by little."

All Kids Understand "Fairness"

"Sometimes people think, Oh, this is so complicated and it will be so hard for my kids to get this. But I always say kids understand the concept of fairness. For example, if their friend gets something and they feel like they deserve it too and they don't get it, what are they going to say? 'That's not fair.' I think that's how you can make any kind of conversation about equality more relatable to them by connecting it to the idea of fairness."

Whether it be through a visit to a historical museum or over everyday meals and car rides, we must have these types of conversations with our children. Tiffany's story reflected her matter-of-fact style of having conversations with her Black boy. As I learned during my conversation with my son about sex, there is no perfect time. When a fertile conversation topic presents itself, it's important to plant a seed. And be mindful that it's just that—a seed. Our children will, for the most part, not be fully blooming with understanding after one or even several conversations. It has to be watered and nourished over time. I also don't assume that I can be the only person tending to their information garden. I know I don't have all the answers and I admit it aloud to my children. When I admit that I don't know something, they let their guards down and we inquire and explore together. My children's favorite go-to for finding answers is "Siri, what is xyz?" While Siri is not always reliable, I know there are other folks in our village who provide droplets of wisdom to nurture their learning, including my brilliant sister Tiffany.

Liberated Parenting Strategy

Reflect

What conversations are around you that you are missing/avoiding? Echoing Tiffany, conversations about isms are not one-day conversations but should happen regularly. And there are opportunities all around us to make connections. Look at where you live: Are there conversations you can have about poverty or privilege? Look at your community: Are there conversations you can have about race and demographics?

Practice

Next time you are driving or eating lunch or dinner with your child(ren), ask them what they notice about their surroundings and how it compares or contrasts with other communities or neighborhoods they are familiar with. Use this conversation as an opportunity to introduce an ism or other societal reality. You can help prepare yourself for the conversation by watching documentaries or reading books such as Beverly Daniel Tatum's *Why Are All the Black Kids Sitting Together in the Cafeteria? And Other Conversations about Race*. Search for articles and blogs for having conversations like these in an age-appropriate way.

Underground Railroad Museum

While Tiffany shows us ways to use the happenings of everyday life to engage in conversations about oppression, there are also ways to engage in these conversations with direct intentionality. During the summer of 2017, I traveled to Kentucky with my son and my mom to visit my paternal family for the first time since I was a child. While on the border between Ohio (free state) and Kentucky (former slave state), we visited the Underground Railroad Museum to learn the rich history of slavery and freedom in the land and to learn about enslaved people who escaped to freedom through Kentucky—where our family is from.

At the museum, there is an exhibit of Henry Box Brown, a former enslaved man who shipped himself to freedom in a cargo box. While engaging in an intimate dialogue with Terrence to demonstrate the severity of this man's journey but also the resilience and creative will involved in the pursuit of freedom, a white patron interrupts me and attempts to whitesplain the story to Terrence, saying, "You know he had to stay in this box for a long journey . . ."

Later in the exhibition, Terrence climbs into the replica cargo box, and while inside the box, the same white patron grabs her camera—ready, uncapped, and loaded—and asks Terrence, "Can I take a photo of you in the box?" This is her second time interrupting our experience, and again she is not talking to me as his mother—she speaks directly to him.

Although my son wants to give her permission to take his photo, I am adamant that she cannot. Later, I explain to Terrence why she couldn't take a picture of him in this box—because I do not need anyone, a white woman particularly, walking around with an image of my son that memorializes slavery with his body. I don't want his body on display for other people. He is not a part of this exhibit; he is not for her entertainment. He is not for her own awakening. His body is not to be disposable or used for her purposes. I also try to explain to him that slavery is a serious crime against our ancestors, and nobody should sentimentalize or sensationalize it.

Liberated Parenting Strategy

Reflect

Connect with historical leaders and heroes by reading books such as *Young, Gifted and Black* by Jamia Wilson. I had the pleasure of interviewing Jamia about her book for the podcast, and she described this work as being guided by love. She wrote this book, which features fifty-two Black leaders, as a love letter from our ancestors to us and from us to the future generation. The title of the book is also the title of a song written and performed by Nina Simone as a love letter to her dear friend Lorraine Hansberry. Similarly, the introductory episode for Parenting for Liberation's podcast series is a letter to my son, Terrence, as a nod to James Baldwin's opening letter to his nephew in *The Fire Next Time*.

Now is your turn to write a letter to your child(ren)! Listen or watch Nina Simone sing "To Be Young, Gifted, and Black" with Black boys and girls on *Sesame Street* in 1972. Write a letter telling them how you see them as young, gifted, and Black. What do you want them to know about themselves, their lineage, their ancestry, and their possibilities for the future? *"There's a world waiting for you, yours is a quest that's just begun."*

Practice

VISITING HISTORICAL SITES OF AFRICAN AMERICAN HISTORY

I encourage you to visit sites of Black history—because that's where it's at. Take your children to museums, read stories about our history, and ask them critical questions.

○ Before visiting a site, have conversations with your kids about African American history regularly. Don't let your visit to the site be your first conversation about history.

○ If discussing enslavement, focus on resistance to enslavement. Speak to the powerful rebellions that took place so that Black children can celebrate the power of their ancestors.

○ Don't begin talking about African American history with slavery—explore history before the transatlantic slave trade.

○ Following the visit, have a Parenting for Liberation O.P.E.N. conversation with your children—create space for them to talk about their feelings.

Kitchen Convos

I n my experience, state violence has a way of arriving on your front doorstep. In the summer of 2016, just a few months before my interview with Cecilia Caballero (see Story 12), two Black men were shot and killed by US police officers within one day of each other. Philando Castile was shot in Minnesota during a routine traffic stop with his girlfriend and her four-year-old daughter in the car, and Alton Sterling was shot while selling CDs and DVDs outside a convenience store in Baton Rouge, Louisiana. Both murders were caught on camera and both of their videos went viral. I refused to watch the videos of the killings for my own self-care because of the vicarious trauma of witnessing Black people under siege, but I had unknowingly stumbled upon the Philando video on Facebook. While cooking dinner and asking my children about their days at school, I found out that my teenage daughter had watched the video on her cell phone. I wasn't prepared to discuss it, but the moment had arrived. Because the topics connected, I shared the experience I had with my daughter with Cecilia. Here is a small clip of the story I shared:

"I was cooking dinner with my children and having a regular conversation about racism and stereotypes, when Ariyah [my daughter] told me that she had watched the videos of Philando Castile's and Alton Sterling's murders at the hands of the state. I was surprised that she'd seen the videos—though this should have been expected, since teenagers have the news at their fingertips with smartphones—and I wasn't prepared to discuss it. I had made a choice not to watch Alton's video after being devastated by the Philando video. Finding out that she watched these very traumatic videos of violence, I got concerned for her and was curious about her experience.

"First, we talked about the cop who murdered Philando Castile, and she had some empathy for him: 'He was like emotionally shook that he had did that. So I don't think he did it on purpose. Like maybe he did on accident.' Being an activist who supports Black Lives Matter, the hairs on the back of my neck were starting to stand up—inside, I wanted her to be as upset and enraged as I was—but externally I validated her understanding. Then I pushed a bit, asking her to reflect on the role of implicit bias and what might have been different if Philando was a white man. 'The cop wouldn't have had his gun out. Because Philando was Black, there are stereotypes. They think that all of us [Black people] are gangsters.'

"Similar to how people try to blame victims for their own murders, Ariyah was curious about the legality of their actions. She asked, 'Was it legal for Philando to carry a gun? Why is it illegal to sell CDs on the street?' Again, I asked her to push past the good versus bad, legal versus illegal Black stereotypes and tropes to help her understand the bigger picture. Philando Castile had a gun permit to carry and he took proper protocol to notify the officer. Alton Sterling had the store owner's permission to sell CDs. But beyond the legalities, I encouraged her to reflect on their human rights and dignity to live and just be. Even if what they were doing was illegal, it shouldn't end in their murder—maybe a ticket or a fine, but it should not have cost them their lives.

"As we closed the conversation I told Ariyah that she, her brother Terrence, Philando, Alton, and all Black people deserve liberation. After she did a glassy-eyed nod, I asked if she knew what liberation meant. When she replied no, I reflected: 'To be liberated is to be free. Free to be yourself. Free to not be afraid when you walk down the street. To walk down the street without worrying about police harassment. Free to just be you. Your loud self. Your quiet self. Your goofy self. Your nerdy self. Your Harry Potter wand–twirling self. Your drama-acting self. Because other kids get to be all of themselves. Then so can you. Black people can just be free. Free to sell CDs (Alton Sterling). Free to drive in their car (Philando Castile). Free to play with toys in the park (Tamir Rice). Free to play loud music (Jordan Davis). Liberation is when we can all be free.'"

Liberated Parenting Strategy

Reflect

In contrast to Tiffany's earlier examples of initiating real conversations with your children in everyday ways, I found myself pulled into a conversation about police violence without any intention or preparation because it just arrived. Sometimes we can't wait for the perfect moment or when we are ready to have conversations. What do you need to prepare yourself for Parenting for Liberation O.P.E.N. conversations with your child(ren) about violence, especially when they have become aware of it themselves? Remember to be open and observant, praise our children's resilience, emote and empathize, and be nonjudgmental and nondirectional.

Practice

While some parents are afraid of scaring their kids because they think that their kids may be too young, as Black parents, it's important to talk to our children. As reflected by my fellow Mama's University mama activist Danielle Slaughter of Mamademics, "Raising children who are knowledgeable of the history and realities of this world does not take away their innocence. It empowers them."

Explore ways to discuss such topics with your children without traumatizing them. For younger children, rather than telling them all the details, share short, concise information followed up with questions for them about how they feel.

Give basic facts (e.g., a young boy was hurt by the police for drawing on the wall) and then ask your child questions:

○   How does that make you feel?
○   Do you feel that was fair?
○   What do you think we can do about it?

For older kids, you can begin to have conversations about why they believe such violence exists and explore the root causes of violence.

No More Police

Cecilia Caballero, cofounder of Chicana M(other)work and coeditor of *The Chicana M(other)work Anthology*

A few months after Parenting for Liberation launched in 2016, I received an affirming message online from Cecilia Caballero. She shared about herself, her son, and the work she was doing with Chicana M(other)work, a group of five mother-scholars who "offer a new interpretation of motherwork that looks at the layers of care work we do in our communities through activism, self-care, teaching, and mothering." As an Afro-Chicana mother, Cecilia reached out and made connections between Parenting for Liberation and Chicana M(other)work that began with a joint podcast, and later grew to us cohosting a track on caregiving and presenting a workshop on Mothering the Revolution at the national Allied Media Conference. Of all our collaborative projects, my favorite was a three-part workshop series for incarcerated mothers at a California women's prison. As a Black feminist impacted by the prison-industrial complex, I entered our curriculum development with the understanding that many of the incarcerated women who would participate in the workshop were more than likely incarcerated due to their own limited "choices"—the constraints of institutional racism, sexism, and classism.

During our podcast with Cecilia, who is a single mother of Alonsito and a PhD candidate at the University of Southern California, we discussed the impact of state violence on our parenting and how to have conversations with our children about it:

"Last week, there was a fourteen-year-old Latino boy named Jesse from the neighborhood where I live in the Eastside of Los Angeles, called Boyle Heights. He was tagging and someone called the police to report the tagging activity. When the police came, he ran, and there's conflicting witness reports of what happened after they arrived. One witness said that he shot a gun at the police, while other witnesses said he did not have a gun. What ended up happening is that he was shot and killed on the street. This happened down the street from where I live. To have police violence or state violence, where a fourteen-year-old was shot in the back and murdered, come so close to my doorstep—I was just having a really hard time. I was talking with my son about it, and he asked me to write down his thoughts to send it to the police. I opened a Google Doc and I wrote down exactly what he said:

No more cops. We don't need you. We need to talk too. Stop arresting, stop killing, stop shooting. You need to apologize. Drop your weapons to the trash. Never kill people again. We need to destroy the police station and make it something else. Whatever we want. Like a space center, dinosaur center, science potions. They cannot keep their station. Police, never do that again."

Liberated Parenting Strategy

Reflect

Cecilia explored alternatives to policing with her son, and you can too. Invite your child(ren) to envision what else is possible instead of violence and surveillance. Ask them: What do you believe is the problem? What is a way to solve the problem?

Practice

Similar to Cecilia, invite your child to make a statement—ask, "If you could say something to police who are violent, what would you say?" If your children are too young to write, have them speak it and you transcribe. Next, if your child wants, you can mail or deliver the letter to the police station.

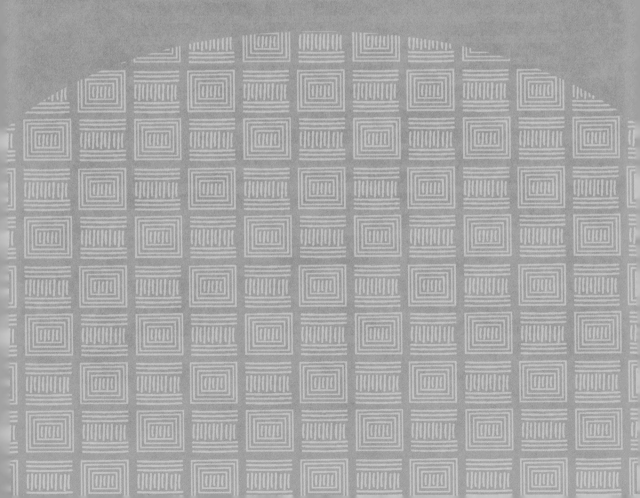

SECTION 3

(Re)connection
to Community

SECTION 3

(Re)connection to Community

Section Three focuses on (re)connection to the broader community. Now that we have had time in Section Two to reconnect with our children as supportive and liberated parents, Section Three explores what supports we need as parents. Parents are often expected to show up and be all things for our children while martyring ourselves. However, as parents we also need support, which can come when we reach out and connect to community. Moreover, as parents for liberation, it's also important that we make connections to the broader movement of Black Liberation as our children's liberation extends beyond our homes. Audre Lorde said, "Raising Black children—female and male—in the mouth of a racist, sexist, suicidal dragon is perilous and chancy. If they cannot love and resist at the same time, they will probably not survive." Thus, connecting to social justice and movement communities is a strategy to raise our children to resist and love.

This section includes stories from Black parents who are actively engaging in community and movement building. These parents are shifting their ways of parenting from an individual and nuclear family structure to an expansive, inclusive, ancestral, and global vision of communal parenting.

Stories in this section will highlight narratives of parents who have explored the ways that we can reconnect to ancestral and African roots of raising our children in a village. Together, we will explore the many sectors of our lives that provide foundations for community building such as faith communities, school communities, movement communities, and global communities. Woven through each story are exercises that engage a variety of reflection approaches including poetry, music, videos, journaling, and art. We want to invite multiple ways of learning. As you do these exercises, notice what is possible for you. Reflect on your community and ask yourself: What are you learning about how you connect with each other? What do you love about your community? Are there any elements of your community that are missing or that you'd like to change?

Finally, the section concludes with an invitation for you to build your own liberated parenting community. There are tools and resources at the back of this book that will show you how to facilitate a Parenting for Liberation session on your own.

STORY 13

Expansive Family Community

Mia Birdsong, former codirector of Family Story

I met Mia Birdsong at a Transitions Lab hosted by the Movement Strategy Center in 2015, before Parenting for Liberation's conception. The Transitions Lab brings together powerful, bold leaders working across distinct but intersecting movements, such as Mia, to explore answers to a key question: How do we transition from a world of domination and extraction to a world of interdependence, resilience, and regeneration? At the time, I was struggling with myself as a parent, and during the lab, it was revealed to me that I had been parenting from fear (using domination). I realized that I needed to transition from parenting for protection to parenting for liberation (and build a relationship with my children rooted in interdependence, resilience, and regeneration).

In addition to kick-starting my journey toward liberation in my parenting, during that lab I met Mia, former codirector of Family Story, which encourages us to push beyond the dominant, mainstream myth of the nuclear family to return to our roots. While we didn't connect for our podcast until over two years later in 2017, she made an impression, not only through her activism but her own parenting. I knew she was a critical voice on how we can expand the ways we build Black families. During my interview with Mia, we discussed the limitations and false narratives that exist about the makeup of the Black family such as extending beyond the traditional nuclear family and paying homage to our African cultural traditions of raising children in a village.

Family Myth

"I am a woman; I'm married to a man. We live in a house and we have a chain-link fence—not a white picket fence—and we're raising our biological children. We get told in America that that's the ideal family structure you should have—and that this family should be self-sufficient and independent. But that doesn't make any sense—it takes way more than two people to raise children. Human beings are pack animals. That setup is a setup for failure.

"What we see right now is so many folks—two grown-ups who are working and trying to raise kids—who get to that place where they ask themselves, Why is it so hard? What am I doing wrong? And I'm like, You're not doing anything wrong. I tell them that this setup is a load of crap.

"My husband and I have never raised our children by ourselves. We have both biological and chosen family who are a significant part of the picture for us, who are taking our kids on outings or picking them up from school or watching them so we can do work or go on dates. It's important for us to have that so that we have more time to take care of ourselves, but it's also important for our kids to have a whole range of adults in their lives who care for them, who show them different ways of being, who introduce them to different things. I would love for us to do an even better job of that. Given how our culture is, it's challenging to try to get people pulled into your circle that way, particularly if they're not biological or legal family. But I think it's really important for us to think expansively about what family is and make sure that for parents and for kids, we have a big bunch of folks who are involved in it."

Busting the Family Myth

"There is a hierarchy in how the dominant discourse defines family. The hierarchy uplifts heterosexual nuclear families; they're usually white in our imagination, they're solidly middle class so they're not dependent on the state, they're independent, and they're raising biological children. This image is deeply embedded in the American dream, where you go to school, meet somebody, fall in love, get married, have babies, and live happily ever after. People think of that idea of family as traditional and there's nothing traditional about it. There was a brief period of time where that was dominant, but even when it was the majority, it was only a small majority. It makes me really sad how the dominant narrative about family, which emphasizes this idea of independence instead of interdependence when it comes to family, is a recipe for disaster. In many ways, I'm trying really hard to not do that.

"Unfortunately, we have this narrative that says that this one kind of nuclear family is the best. All of American cultural norms and our policies and practices are designed to support that kind of family. There's all this faulty, misguided research that says that kids who grow up in those families—families with two married parents—have the best outcome. As a comparison, I always say, for example, if we look at something like the wage gap, men are clearly doing better in the workplace than women when it comes to income, but we all know that that's not because there's something inherently better about men. We know that's because there's this great inequity in terms of how wages are distributed. Similarly, to say that nuclear families are doing better because they're nuclear is ridiculous. What we have is a system that's set up to privilege them. Everything works for them. Everybody else has to navigate around them."

Family Story: Shifting the Narrative

"The work I do with Family Story is to create new narratives about families. So the work that we do is really about telling the celebratory, positive stories about families who are not nuclear families. We try to frame and understand the challenges that families face collectively, which has nothing to do with 'bad choices,' but with the failure of our systems and structures to actually meet all families where they are.

"What works best for kids is to have people who love them and who are stable parts of their lives. What works best for kids is to have access to really good education and stable housing and nutritious food, and to not be poor. None of these have anything to do with family structure but with what we prioritize as a country, and the decisions we've made about allowing people to be poor or allowing kids to go to crappy schools or penalizing people for the kind of family structure that they have."

Cultural Traditions of Family

"We have always had different ways of doing families. We've always had intergenerational families, always had queer families. We've always had matrilineal families, where you have women raising children with their sisters and their mothers. There's invisibility of the different nodes of connection that existed in our families because of the way in which America defines who counts as a family.

"Black folks have a long tradition of doing this. Most of the Black adults that I know have aunties or uncles that we didn't find out weren't actually the siblings of our parents until we were adults. I was talking to a friend the other day who was going through family pictures and there were people who are in their family who they didn't actually know if they were biological family. I just think that's really beautiful that they didn't know and they're like, 'it doesn't matter.' It is really important to have expansive notions of what family is while parenting."

Blueprint for the Next Generation

"I feel like there are a lot of young folks right now who know that what their parents did didn't work. They want to do family in a different way but don't have a lot of narratives that show them what that looks like. I'm really hoping that the stories that we tell will show people that there are different ways to do family than what they grew up with. To provide some blueprints and touchstones and ideas about what it could look like for them to create their own family."

Similar to what Mia shared, I grew up, at times unbeknownst to myself, in an expansive family. I have many family members, play cousins, godsisters, and half sisters that I always considered full. As a child, their biological connection was not as important as the relational connection—how these family members were supportive, were present, and showered me with love. As children we needed that village, and now as parents we need a village of "framily" to support us as we raise liberated children. *Framily* is a term that means friends who are close like family. There is no definitive origin of the word but it has increased in popularity with the prevalence of concepts such as Friendsgiving and chosen family. While becoming popular in the mainstream, the idea of framily has existed in the Black community for some time because we have always had to rely on folks beyond our nuclear family. Too often we are told as Black parents to be all things (mamas, you know the superwoman motif!)—but it's time to break that down and, as Mia said, really begin to amplify the stories of expansive and inclusive definitions of Black family, reclaiming our ancestral ways of community parenting among a village.

Liberated Parenting Strategy

Reflect

Watch or listen to "Blended Family (What You Do For Love)" by Alicia Keys, featuring A$AP Rocky.

As the song notes, blended (expansive and inclusive) framilies are beautiful. Reflect on the beauty of your framily. The song also acknowledges that framilies can get hard. Sometimes there's pain, harm, and disconnection. The song mentions that family doesn't have to be limited to blood relatives—chosen family is important. Who do you choose to be in your family to help you support you and your child(ren)?

Practice

Write a poem about the people in your village. Some of you might be saying, "I'm not a poet!" A strategy to move past writer's block is to play the song (or set a timer for five minutes) and freewrite. Just pick up a pen (if you're old-school) or open a blank document (if you're high-tech) and allow the words to flow out of you. Don't erase, don't edit, don't correct—whatever comes up, put it down on paper. If a prompt would be helpful, you can start with "My village/community/framily is . . ." and just finish the sentence as many times as you can, describing your village/community/framily until the song ends or timer sounds.

Bonus Practice

Once you write your poem about the beauty of your framily village, reach out to those people, tell them how much you appreciate them being in your life.

Communities of Faith

Ida McRae, social worker

The year 2017 brought increased repressive policies such as the Muslim travel ban initiated by the Trump administration, and in 2019 we saw heightened violence against Muslim communities during the attack in Christchurch, New Zealand, that left over fifty dead and fifty more injured. We often forget that African Americans make up nearly one-third of the US Muslim community, and we often don't hear about the experiences of Black Muslims. I asked Chelsey, a Muslim friend of mine, to connect me with one of her Muslim sisters who is also parenting, and she connected me with Ida McRae, a Black Muslim parent and social worker who strives to support the social and emotional well-being of her community. Ida does a lot of work to destigmatize mental health for communities of color and Muslim families while also striving to raise a beautiful Black Muslim girl to love both her Blackness and her faith, and combating both anti-Blackness and Islamophobia. Here is a snippet of what Ida shared with me during our conversation:

Black and Muslim

"When I think about being a Black Muslim woman and parent, I think primarily about being a Black person in the United States and that history and trauma I have experienced just with carrying that one identity. Sometimes adding the other identities of woman and Muslim kind of feels like an added experience of aggression here. But it also feels like a very great experience to have in terms of community and history.

"There is an inaccurate perception of what the Muslim community is here in the United States; however, it's interesting when you see the statistics, where nearly one-third of the Muslim community here is Black. Yet when you look at the media, you don't see that same representation. As a Black Muslim woman, my experience is oftentimes ignored. On the other hand, you see so many Black women and Black men who are Muslim, who are trailblazers, who are doing amazing things here to shift that narrative and create that type of representation."

Anti-Blackness in the Muslim Community

"Even sometimes within the Muslim community, we face racism, internalized racism, and bigotry. You can be in a space where everyone around you is Brown or Black, but the sentiments that they have toward African Americans are misguided. That can sometimes be a conflicting experience, because you're around people who share the same faith. However, sometimes you're being harmed in some of those spaces, either by things that people say or imply or by the absence and lack of acknowledgment of your experience. I was leading a group for Black Muslim girls around social justice activism and identity development, and we had an organization that does amazing work around civil rights within the Muslim community come out and speak about ways to empower Muslim youth within school settings and what rights we have here as Muslims. None of the pamphlets or marketing material had even one family within their brochures that was Black. Then combine the lack of representation with having to deal with folks' internalized oppression and their assimilation into white racist culture."

Xenophobia in the African American Community

"When I'm in Black communities, I have experienced Islamophobia and xenophobia. First, there is this belief that there's no way I can be African American. Some folks may be assuming that I'm not African American because I wear a hijab, so they think that I'm from somewhere else. That can be an isolating experience; however, what I realized is, some people just don't know. Many are adopting certain ideas and thoughts that they see on television. Sometimes it's shocking, because there are so many African American Muslims in this country. When you think about trailblazers, folks who stood up for Islam and were unapologetically Muslim in this country, many of them were historically African Americans. Furthermore, when you think about the Africans who were brought here centuries ago, some of our ancestors were brought here as Muslims and were indoctrinated to take on other religions. It's a very interesting experience that can be conflicting and it can sometimes even be isolating. However, once we get to know one another—share space and stories with one another—then it can really break down the ice. I realize then how much we have in common, especially as Black people here in the United States."

Finding Community in Wholeness

"There are many people like me who share the same experience and identity, but it took me a while to kind of get to a point where I feel content about those experiences. That really was through prayer but also traveling, traveling to different states throughout the country and interacting with different Muslim communities and being around certain African American, Black-predominant Muslim communities in the nation. One example is Sapelo Square, which is an online resource for Black Muslims and is a great forum that really centers Black Muslim narratives. Just seeing how beautiful, organized, and proud the various communities are makes me realize that is something that I can create for myself and for my daughter moving forward.

"In terms of creating a space where you're able to parent in a liberated manner and connect with other Black families, as a parent, I want my daughter to feel empowered and feel proud of all of her identities and to be able to be in those spaces and to say, 'I am Black. I am Muslim, I am here and this is my narrative and my story.' Also, regardless of faith, I think we have a lot more in common than we have differences. I think the focus should really be on tolerating each other, learning from each other, and organizing with each other, because the more that we're divided the easier it is for us to be taken advantage of. If we were to come together as Black folks from a variety of backgrounds and intersections, we would have so much power and strength. People talk about self-care a lot, but sometimes that puts so much responsibility on an individual. I think it's beyond self-care. I think it's also community care."

Standing in Solidarity

"There's a couple of strategies that come to mind, and one of them is highlighting Black Muslim heroes, historical figures, and trailblazers as a part of Black American history in general. For example Malcolm X, but then also more contemporary folks that we might see in the media like Movita Johnson-Harrell, the first Muslim woman elected state representative in Pennsylvania; Ilhan Omar, the first Somali American, first African-born American, and one of the first two Muslim American women to serve in the US Congress; and Ibtihaj Muhammad, the first American to compete at the Olympics in a hijab and the first Muslim American woman to win a medal.

"Inform your children that this is a part of our history as Black people in this nation. As it relates to younger children, teach tolerance of diverse beliefs. Learn basics about Islamic faith and don't just believe what you see on television, the negative propaganda around Muslims. Because that same machine that's spreading hate is the same machine that spreads hate around Black folks and immigrants and a variety of communities. It's the same system that's really dividing people, demeaning people, and dehumanizing folks. We can counter that by teaching tolerance. Learn about the folks that are your neighbors, that go to school with you, and really stand in solidarity with them. Reach out to the Black Muslims that you may know. Disrupt Islamophobia and microaggressions that are in school settings, at home, and at work, where these comments and these experiences are happening around us in a variety of settings. Be that person to challenge and name an offensive comment. Even if you're the only person to say it, being courageous in that moment can really show your solidarity."

> "Be that person to challenge and name an offensive comment. Even if you're the only person to say it."
> —IDA MCRAE

During my conversation with Ida, we explored the critical role of faith and spirituality as a source of sustaining, healing, and resilience within Black communities. As someone who was raised Christian, faith has always been central to my belief in possibilities, hope for the future, and commitment to liberation. Lately, I have been embarking on a journey to reclaim and reconnect to ancestral practices of spirituality to help fortify me on my path toward liberation. I have been practicing ancestral African spiritual traditions such as pouring libations and calling on my ancestors, and singing the old Negro spirituals used in slave resistance and rebellion such as "Swing Low, Sweet Chariot." Ida reminded me that although I, like many other millennials, am broadening my faith to include African traditions, I should also acknowledge and remember the historical and current roles of faith traditions in our struggles for freedom. For example, the Black church was foundational to the civil rights movement with leaders such as Reverend Martin Luther King Jr. The Muslim faith and Nation of Islam, with leaders such as Malcolm X and the Honorable Elijah Muhammad, were and have been key to the Black nationalist movement. I honor the role of faith and spirit in our fight for liberation.

STORY
14

Liberated Parenting Strategy

Reflect

Read *Bashirah and the Amazing Bean Pie: A Celebration of African American Muslim Culture*. This book is an invitation to our children to enjoy the rich and beautiful culture of African American Muslims. *Bashirah and the Amazing Bean Pie* shares a fantastic story of a multigenerational African American Muslim family, a heart-warming tale filled with faith, food, and family. After reading the book, reflect on what your family traditions are for holidays, celebrations, grieving, etc. As Ida said, we have more in common than we have differences. What are the connections you can make? How are your practices similar to the Muslim culture described in the story? After learning more about Black Muslim culture, are there any stereotypes or misinformation that you are unlearning?

Practice

Learn about the Muslim community. Ida recommended Sapelo Square, an online resource whose mission is to celebrate and analyze the experiences of Black Muslims in the United States to create new understandings of who they are, what they have done, and why that matters. Upon visiting their site, you can learn about the meaning of their name:

> We take the name "Sapelo" from one of the first communities of African Muslims in the United States founded in the early 1800s. On Sapelo Island, off the coast of Georgia, enslaved African Muslims struggled to hold on to their Islamic roots amidst the dehumanizing institution of slavery. Like the celebrated Congo Square of New Orleans, we take the name "square" in reference to the town square as a community space and a cultural hub for African-descended people.

Explore the Sapelo Square webpage and learn about the issues impacting our Black Muslim brothers and sisters. What are the connections you can make to your own experience?

Bonus Practice

Build within and across community. Ida reflected on her experiences of Islamophobia and xenophobia as a Black Muslim woman from other Black folks within Black communities. She made a call for the Black community to stand in solidarity with our Black Muslim brothers and sisters and provided many examples: learn about the folks that are your neighbors, teach tolerance, disrupt Islamophobia and microaggressions, learn basics about Islamic faith, highlight Black Muslim heroes, historical figures, and trailblazers as a part of Black American history.

Of the list of solidarity strategies that Ida provided, which can you engage in first? In addition to doing the external work of solidarity, it also takes internal work. We must first reflect on our own behaviors and beliefs. Reflect on your own narratives about Muslim culture—are there any negative stereotypes or beliefs that you need to unpack?

Global Communities

Monalisa Oluko Diallo, educator

I was connected to Monalisa Oluko Diallo through China Martens, one of the coeditors of *Revolutionary Mothering* and a fierce ally to mothers of color. Monalisa—who China described as a Baltimore mother, grandmother, teacher, community gardener, and radical example for many—worked as a paraeducator for Baltimore County for over twenty years. In our conversation, she shared that her life purpose was to raise independent, discerning, loving, competent humans, and one of her strategies was raising globally conscious children. She raised her own children across the globe from Europe to Baltimore to Japan. Here is a slice of the brilliance that Monalisa shared with me:

Life through Travel

"I realize that when I travel, I very rarely see any families traveling together. But my sons have traveled all over the world. My youngest son went to South Africa when he was fifteen years old and he came back with a very interesting perspective. Then my daughter attended college in West Africa and she came back with a very enlightened approach on life. So I would say to parents, 'Please be compelled to take your children and show them life through travel.' If you celebrate the holidays, make that a gift, an experience. I know some parents that are like, 'I gotta get this iPad or the latest thing.' But there is nothing, in my opinion, that can ever surpass giving your children great experiences.

"It reminds me of a story of a woman here in Baltimore. She said she had an agreement with their son not to have cable for a year. She said her cable bill was around $250 or something ridiculous and needed to save that money. If they could save all of their money, she would match it and she would take them out of the country.

"If it is possible for you to take your children out of the country (and not just a retreat on a beach), take them to see how other people live. Have conversations with mothers and their children in marginalized and disenfranchised communities. When I was in Jamaica for the first time, I stayed in the hills with a host family. Every morning at about five o'clock, there were children that had to fill their buckets with water and walk back home to the washroom to have it ready for the morning. I asked why the watering hole was not on. They told me that it's because all the water goes toward the tourist areas and they get water intermittently and don't get water all the time. You have people that go to the resort and always have water and everything else, but there are other communities that are suffering."

Local to Global

"We can teach our children in our own neighborhoods as well. Every time I got paid, I would take my children to a restaurant that was not our typical restaurant. I would go to a Senegalese or Ethiopian restaurant and we would have a day of learning. We learned about Ethiopia or Senegal: Where it is? Who are the people? What language do they speak? You can do that as a parent in an urban area and it really doesn't cost that much."

As Mona reflected on the story of the Baltimore mom who canceled cable television to save money for an international trip, it was a mindset shift. I was curious if my lack of travel as a child was about mindset or something else. As an adult, I asked my mom why we didn't travel, and she reflected that during her own childhood she didn't have many opportunities to travel. Because she wasn't allowed to travel, let alone go out with her friends (she often tells me the story of how she was not allowed to leave the front yard as a kid), she grew up with a fear of the unknown. This fear can be transmitted

"Take your children and show them life through travel."
—MONALISA OLUKO DIALLO

from generation to generation; however, I am making a conscious effort to push past generational fear and provide my children with opportunities to move, explore, and be free. Because of the nature of my work, I am afforded opportunities to travel and took my son on his first work flight at three years old. It wasn't until 2019 that we had an international trip, which was a short cruise from Los Angeles to Mexico. As Mona reflected, it is not just about distance—you can also visit local communities that are different than your regular environment. Here in Los Angeles, we have Little Ethiopia, Koreatown, Chinatown, etc. If you don't have the means or you are limited in your ability to travel due to medical issues or lack of documentation, read in the strategy section for practical advice on how to explore and learn inside and outside of your neighborhood with your kids.

Wherever you travel, whether near or far, be intentional about using your travel to explore the context and histories of the places you are visiting. This past summer, when my work called me to Montgomery, Alabama, I took my son with me because of the historical context of being in the South. While there, we went to the Riverfront, where we learned that thousands of enslaved Africans arrived by boat and were chained together, paraded up Commerce Street, and sold on auction blocks. Together, my son and I traced the paths of our ancestors, walked to the river, and honored their legacy. My son picked up a stone he found by the river and said, "This is for our ancestors. This rock is hard and strong. Take this rock as an appreciation for fighting for our freedom." As he tossed it into the water he said, "If you're out there, thanks."

Liberated Parenting Strategy

Reflect

Mona shared some ideas about local to global activities that folks can engage their children with to learn new cultures and broaden their horizons. Look up local restaurants or museums that represent and reflect different African cultures. Before visiting the establishment, research the culture, people, their beliefs, values, language, and history. Write a list of the local field cultural hubs you will visit with your child (e.g., museums, cultural centers, restaurants). Mona also shared that there is local diversity all around you in your neighbors, classmates, and friends. Talk to the folks around you and learn more about their cultural heritage.

Practice

International travel can be expensive, and many families feel like it's out of reach. What would be possible if we didn't buy the latest tennis shoes or gadget? Are there other experiential gifts that could provide our children with lifelong experiences versus temporary toys, items, or electronics? And if you do take a trip, before traveling to a place, talk to your children about the community you are visiting. Research and learn about the language, food, history, traditions, etc. Check out these online resources on traveling while Black such as: The MOM Trotter, Black Kids Do Travel, and Travel Noire.

Bonus Practice

Mona also reflected on international travel as an opportunity to learn and give back, not only for luxury and recreation. As you travel, particularly if you are from the United States or other privileged countries visiting underserved communities, it's important to have an understanding that the wealth of the United States was built on the backs of Black people and other people of color across the globe. While visiting other countries impacted by colonization, try to have an anti-capitalist approach (not about what you can get/extract from others), and instead make sure your visit is centered on values of interdependence and giving back. As you visit, ask yourself, What can I give to the communities I visit?—not as a charity worker but as an effort to build a global community. And when I say give back, I mean broadened beyond monetary or tangible items, so gifts of time, support, a helping hand, a song, a poem, a ritual, a chant, a prayer, a meal—gifts from you and your child(ren)'s heart to their global brothers and sisters.

Exploring Liberated Educational Spaces

Dia Penning, founder of The Equity Collective

Many of our children spend the majority of their day at school. While we cultivate liberation in our homes, it's important that we also find liberated school environments that support our children. The following three stories reflect the conversations that parents and educators have regarding liberated schools.

In 2017 I joined the Network Weaver Learning Lab (yeah, I know, I participate in a lot of labs—I'm a lifelong learner), which brings together California leaders to experiment together on ways to advance the movement to end relationship-based violence. It was there that I met Dia Penning, and we hit it off, connecting about raising Black boys and our intentional search for them to be in liberated learning environments. Rather than waiting until I got home to interview her, Dia and I hung out in our dorm-style room, used our cell phones, and began recording our conversation. By the time our eighteen-month lab came to an end, Dia and I had made a video interview sharing the ingredients of recipes for liberated parent-child relationships. Here is some of what Dia shared during our conversation:

Liberated School

"The school that my son attends has the philosophy that if the teachers are liberated, the children will be liberated. It's run by a teacher collective; there's no head of school. Everything is decided by consensus. It has created an environment where children have as much agency as the adults at the school. The children are really able to be a partner in their education. What's so interesting is that in that environment, he gets a choice. He's in a space where if he has to use the bathroom, he gets to go to the bathroom. He doesn't have to ask anybody. He doesn't get the third degree if he's been gone for more than two minutes. He gets to make a choice about whether or not he wants to play inside or outside. He gets to choose which book he wants to read. He's able to make up stories that come from his imagination. He's able to tell stories that come from his imagination instead of the teacher calling him out."

Find a school that helps to liberate your child. Negotiate with the administration in order to get your kid into that school. You don't have to settle for something that's not working for you.

See Themselves in Their Teacher

"In the grand scheme of things, it's not the most diverse place that we could have sent him, but he is definitely not the only person of color. Half of the teaching staff are people of color. He's not the only kid of color. His kindergarten teacher is an African American woman, has raised two children. She has been teaching for forty-five years and she loves her children and she especially loves her Black children. Not only is it a space that liberates all of the children, but it's a place that holds Black children in a very particular way that allows them to flourish and see themselves."

Options

"This was not the opportunity that we were going to have at the public school near our house or at the charter school that was around the corner. It just wasn't. Keep in mind that I'm an educator—I've worked in elementary schools and high schools—and I know that teachers work really hard. I know that they're constantly combating their own unconscious bias. I know that they are committed to kids, but I think that there is something to be said for liberating the teachers to do the job of teaching without making them responsible for test scores, without making them responsible for managing a classroom of thirty kids, without making them responsible for things that take away from them doing their jobs as teachers.

White Women and School Pushout

"I think that there are probably white women teachers that are totally fueling the school-to-prison pipeline based on their own fear and misunderstanding of Black boys in particular. Black girls as well. They're misunderstanding how we express intimacy, how we express anger, what trust looks like for us. I think that there is a complete disconnect, and I think that they believe that they are doing the best that they can. White supremacy is so deeply encoded in our DNA that even people that believe that they are woke still perpetuate harm."

STORY 16

Liberated Parenting Strategy

Reflect

Instead of trying to make our kids fit into traditional learning environments like cookie cutters, cultivate Black brilliance that breaks the mold. What are some boxes your child(ren) are breaking out of? How are you supporting and encouraging your child(ren) to break out of boxes and boundaries that limit their creativity and brilliance?

Practice

Sometimes we are cultivating our children's liberation in our home, but sending them to school environments can stifle it, so one thing that I do each year is send a letter or email to my child's teachers as soon as the school year begins. This helps to ensure that we are on the same page about cultivating his Black brilliance. Here is a sample letter I send:

1. Introduce yourself and why you are reaching out.

   My name is Trina. I am the proud mother of Terrence, who is in your class this year. Over the past couple of years, I have found it helpful to partner closely with his teachers to find strategies to help him succeed in the classroom and at home. I am reaching out to give you a little background about Terrence, his strengths and areas for support to ensure you have the information needed for a successful school year.

2. Introduce your child, sharing all the amazing things that the teacher can look forward to!

Terrence will bring you and your class so much joy and happiness. He has a huge heart that he wears on his sleeves—he is very friendly, compassionate, and empathetic. Ask any of his previous teachers and they will rave about how sweet of a boy he is. He is a total jokester and will make folks laugh without even trying. He is smart and intuitive and has a unique way of seeing the world. He can show you a new way to see things if you let him, and don't limit his imagination. He's an innovator and creator, and loves solving problems by doing.

3. Express the best ways to support your child, making note of strategies that did/didn't work in the past.

Because he is such an empathetic boy, he takes criticism personally and hates being scolded publicly. He won't always let you know it, but he worries and is very sensitive. It will be best to pull him aside and give him his feedback. In addition to learning by doing, Terrence is also very social and loves to be in conversations about what he is learning. In our home, we are very dyadic communicators, so interactive conversations will come more naturally than raising his hand and waiting his turn.

4. Express any other concerns you may have regarding your child. (Here is where I would speak to concerns around race, culture, etc.)

Beyond learning styles and lesson plans, I want to raise your awareness to the fact that Terrence may be one of the few (or the only)

African American students in your classroom. I hope this is obvious to you and you are not living in a "colorblind society," because our world is not colorblind, it is in fact very racialized, so I want to ensure that this very important cultural competency piece be held with as much rigor as his education and academics. I want Terrence to be proud of his culture and heritage, and I want him to be affirmed for his humanity. Please be mindful of this as you engage with him, as he engages with his peers, as you make choices about structures in class, and as you make choices about assignments, topics, readings, etc. Here are a few articles that I think may be helpful:

- For an article about the ways Black children are criminalized and punished in ways non-Black children aren't, see Valerie Strauss's "Implicit Racial Bias Causes Black Boys to be Disciplined at School More Than Whites, Federal Report Finds."[7]
- For an article about the impact of racism on Black children with disabilities, see Stephanie Keeney Parks's "How Racism Impacts Black Kids with Autism."[8]

5. Conclude with ways you'd like the teacher to engage with you throughout the school year as it pertains to your child.

I have volunteered weekly in each of his classes at his previous school and I look forward to working closely with you. I have also helped his former teachers with ideas around celebrating Black History Month and other culturally relevant curriculum (i.e., around Thanksgiving and honoring the indigenous people of this land). Please contact me at any time by phone or by email. I have a flexible schedule and am able to meet whenever it is convenient for you. Thanks for taking the time to review this email.

Sincerely, Terrence's Mom,
Trina Greene Brown

Visioning Liberated Schools

Mikala Streeter, founder of The LIFE School

I connected with Mikala Streeter online when she reached out to talk about liberated learning institutions. Mikala is the founder of the LIFE School, a self-directed, project-based high school that places freedom, choice, and responsibility in the hands of the person doing the learning. She shared more about the school's philosophy as an example of an alternative school:

"At our school, we encourage our students to explore all of the things that motivate them, intrigue them, and excite them. As adults, we know that over time, you might start with one thing when you're eighteen and then when you're twenty-five, it shifts. Over time as students get more information and have more experiences, these things ebb and flow and change in different ways, and that's okay. But to have something clear when they graduate from high school is the goal. Our school focuses everything we do on how they are building skills—academic, personal, and professional skills—but also how they are having a space to explore their own interests, to get the students to know themselves better while also learning more about the world and broadening their picture of what else is happening around them in their communities, in our country, in the world—all different countries, and cultures, and everything that's out there. Our school encourages them to broaden that picture so they have a clear sense of everything, and they can better find where they fit, where they can make the most impact in all of this."

Liberated Parenting Strategy

Practice

Within each of us, we have a vision of a different world. Invite your child(ren) to envision a liberated school. All you need is some art supplies: construction paper, poster board, markers, crayons, colored pencils, old magazines, and glue. Let your imagination take over! Invite your child(ren) on a guided visioning.

Imagine you are arriving to a liberated school:

○ What is the first thing you see—What does the building look like? What color is the building? What is the shape of the building? What else do you see?

○ You enter the school and you are walking around the campus— What do you see? What do you feel? What do you hear? What do you smell?

○ You see the teachers and principals—What do they look like? What do they say? How do they speak to you? How do they make you feel?

○ You see other students—What do they look like? What do they say? What's their personality like? What do they care about? What do they do for fun?

○ The school day begins—How do you spend your day? Are you in classrooms? How is the classroom set up? What are you learning throughout the day? What are the topics you discuss? What are the books you are reading? Who are the main characters in the books? Who are the authors of the books? Does the material reflect you? How do your teachers teach you? What is your schedule for breaks?

○ Lunch time—What are your meal options? How does the food taste? Is it nutritious? Is there enough for everyone? Do you feel full and ready to continue learning?

Imagining Liberated Futures

Jacqueline Roebuck Sakho, founder of
Black Activist Mothering

Though we connected virtually first, the universe brought Jacqueline Roebuck Sakho and I together in Detroit in February 2017. Danielle Atkinson, executive director of Mothering Justice, invited both Jacqueline and I, along with other badass Black mother activists, to develop Mama's University, an online learning fellowship for mothers of color. Jacqueline is the founder of Black Activist Mothering and has been a trailblazer in the fields of restorative justice and community-based educational leadership. She has also been radically parenting six children over the last twenty years. Here is what Jacqueline shared during our conversation about educational institutions and the limits they place on Black children's brilliance:

Kindergarten Pushout

"As soon as we place our children into the public school system, they're negotiating and navigating that at five. I came into an elementary school where a young Black sister was the principal to do consulting with a community-based organization that was providing an alternative to the discipline program. We were working with the fourth, fifth, and sixth graders; however, I had to walk by the kindergarten class to get to the fifth graders. While walking by, I see this little brilliant Black boy sitting out at the table—everything about him just made me want to hug him and love him up. I go over there and I ask, 'Why are you sitting out here?' And he said, 'My teacher said I don't follow instructions.' I said, 'You're five, what do you mean you don't follow instructions?' He said, 'Well, I'm supposed to trace these letters.' I took him with me to the office, where he took a business card, looked at it one time, and then recited it back to me and wrote the name and numbers from the business card. I said, 'Well, we're going to find something else to do,' because he was way beyond tracing letters. His ability was far beyond tracing letters as his teacher assigned. He came to school ready to do bigger and greater work, but the system isn't designed for that.

"This is how school pushout starts, this is how the discipline issue starts as early as kindergarten—when a teacher, a white teacher, decides that the classroom is their space and the student does not belong if he doesn't comply. However, the teacher's role is as a public servant in a public school. This space belongs to the children and their families. What are you going to do to ensure that this child stays in his space?

"I'm not even saying that this only happens with white teachers, because Baltimore taught us that you can have an entirely Black school and still have a high rate of discipline disparity for Black kids. It's really about how are you performing whiteness, how are you performing white supremacy, even if you're not white?"

Liberated Parenting Strategy

Reflect

Jacqueline reflected on the role of racism in schools and how whiteness and white supremacy can be performed by people of color. In my work, I've learned from racial equity teachers Monica Dennis and Rachael Ibrahim about the ways that not only white folks internalize racial superiority but also people of color internalize racial inferiority. One of the readings for organizational work was "The Characteristics of White Supremacy Culture" from *Dismantling Racism: A Workbook for Social Change Groups* by Kenneth Jones and Tema Okun, which I applied to my own personal habits in my home. For example, the habit of perfectionism was linked to my enforcing respectability with our children (e.g., telling our sons to "pull your pants up" or telling our girls to be "ladylike"). How can we as Black parents perform white supremacist expectations on our own children in an effort to ensure their safety and success?

Practice

"What would the world look like if we allowed our black children to be as free as their white peers? If we encouraged their inquisitiveness and impulsiveness instead of telling them to be quiet, get in line, and

follow instructions? Maybe, just maybe, we would have the blueprint to the next revolution." —Danielle Moodie-Mills, *"OpEd: Does the Revolution Begin with a Free Black Child?"*

Imagine what it would be like if our children didn't have to conform to white ideals. Spend some time imagining how you would raise your child(ren) if you weren't concerned about the white gaze.

Afrofuturism Letter Writing

Imagine forty to fifty years from now, and your children have had children. Or think even further into the future—of your grandchildren's children. Imagine you are receiving a letter from one of your (great-)grandchildren that describes a world where Black children can, as Danielle Moodie-Mills puts it, "be as free as their white peers." The letter thanks you, specifically for the choices you made to be a liberated parent to their own parent or grandparent.

Grab a sheet of paper, play some reflective music, and begin writing a letter to yourself from the perspective of one of your future (great-)grandchildren. Here are prompts to get you started:

- How do they describe their world? What is possible for them?
- What does their daily life look like?
- How do they learn? Are there schools or a different educational structure?
- How is their relationship with their parents? Siblings? Community?
- What do they care about?

Bonus Practice

Let's focus on gratitude. What does your (great-)grandchild thank you for? What did you do to make this possible? What were the shifts you made?

Sample Future Letters:

WRITTEN BY THE DESCENDANTS OF TRINA GREENE BROWN:

Dear Mama Akua,

Greetings and blessings from Ghana. Your voyage here thirty years ago planted seeds for our commune here where we live collectively as family within larger community. Each sunrise we awake with morning prayers off the coast in four directions, honoring our ancestors and elders who sacrificed for us to return home. Here the children are sacred, and their most important role is to simply be children, to play, and be loved. They learn stories, songs, and the land. Even the smallest child can tell which foods and herbs grown provide healing. Parents are communal and collective. We all parent regardless of biological connection.

WRITTEN BY THE DESCENDANTS OF LESLI LEGRAS MORRIS:

Dear Queen Mother,

Wakanda is amazing. Yesterday at school, we had an art/tech fair, and I got to show off my new discovery—an herb that counters the effects of body weathering due to the racism your generation and our ancestors endured across the diaspora. It's already shown promise of ending maternal mortality and tons of other ailments and diseases that our community faces.

WRITTEN BY THE DESCENDANTS OF JESSICA ROSS:

Dear Sugar Love,

I love you dearly. Thank you, Sugar, for fighting, loving, and resisting. It's so beautiful here amongst the stars. Sugar Love, you would be so proud. We are taught love of self and respect, and we honor you, our ancestors, who have paved the way. Thank you for your act of love, your resistance, and your courage. It's so free here. The liberation you wanted to see. Kids are not taught in classrooms. They are able to nurture their interests and talents, to be their best selves.

STORY 19

Movement Communities

Johnaé Strong, member of BYP100

During an Innovation Lab I was cohosting, I met creative spirit and BYP100 member Je Naé Taylor, who wrote a chant I had been singing for months called "I Love Being Black." When I fangirled out about the song, Je Naé shared with me that an entire album full of chants and songs celebrating Black joy was coming out in a couple months. I was lit! I told her that I wanted to highlight the album when it dropped by interviewing a parent who participated in the recording. Je Naé connected me with Johnaé Strong and the rest is history. Johnaé is a Black mommy of two—six-year-old Akeim and two-year-old Jari—as well as an educator and organizer dedicated to healing and liberation for all Black people. During the interview, we discussed her work on *The Black Joy Experience* album that was released by BYP100 in summer 2018. This album features a musical collection dedicated to freedom songs and liberation chants that keeps joy at the center of the fight for Black Liberation. She also reflected on the role of caregivers and children in the movement, and how we must be willing to be transformed in service of the work for the sake of liberation. Here is an excerpt of what Johnaé shared during our conversation:

Raised in the Movement

"A lot of the work that we do comes from our experience in the world—for me, being a Black mother to two children. Akeim is basically the same age as the organization, BYP100. I was actually at the original convening of the one hundred that was the pretext to the organization, and because I was newly having my son, every time we grow a year older, so does my son, who was literally raised in the movement. A lot of the songs and chants that are on the BYP100's *Black Joy Experience* album are chants that my son and I, along with our comrades and our family, have done together."

I Love Being Black

"When it came down to actually recording the album, it was full of beautiful moments, because my son was surrounded by his movement family—his uncle John, me his mom, his tete Val—and we're just singing and chanting these affirmations around his Blackness. It was just the most beautiful experience ever. One of the sessions for the recording was in New Orleans, and that's just a very deeply rich Black spiritual place—I mean just every experience around this album has brought me joy, even just in the process of making it. It's very, very cool to know that now people are able to enjoy it and people are able to be in their car listening to it. You know, I love Black people. The other really cool thing is that there's other caretakers in BYP100—one is Ife Williams. Akeim refers to Ife's son Khamari as his brother. I just remember them and another little girl, Sophia, doing the chant down in New Orleans. It was the most beautiful thing ever. It was one of those moments where I felt like the work I'm doing is important. Yes, we got this policy passed or were able to have an officer held accountable for violence against Black people—but really when you see three Black children chanting and singing, 'I love being Black,' that's what it's all about."

My Children Teach Me How to Have Joy

"I really feel like the energy of caretakers and mamas in movement spaces is so critical, so sacred, and so valuable. You have a human being that you have to be accountable to—whether they eat, they are clothed, they are able to get an education; and all of these systems are directly impacting this human life that has no say-so in the way that their life is presented to them. It keeps you vigilant and it keeps you passionate. The other piece which is very much important as well is that my children teach me how to have joy. They teach me when I need healing. For example, if I'm coming home and I'm stressed out and I'm cranky with them and they're trying to play and I'm not really paying attention, they let me know. Like, 'Mom, you need to check in. You need to chill out. You need to do something that's not so heavy and burdensome and enjoy the ability to live life.' They teach me how to have a lot of gratitude, lightheartedness, and a lot of joy.

"In this movement work, I have been transformed, because I have these two beautiful little people with me every step of the way. I'm much more accountable to my own health and wellness than I ever was when I first started organizing, because initially, I was organizing to topple the systems of patriarchy, capitalism, racism. However, I was much less cognizant of the very inner work of healing. How do I get back the energy that I need to keep going into the struggle? Creating an opportunity to take a moment to care for myself and other people? Truly honoring my own humanity even as I'm doing this work?"

Power of Children and Caregivers in Movement Spaces

"There's an energy and a spirit that comes with the relationship between the caretaker and a child, and when they're present in movement spaces, I noticed many times that people become more gentle in the space, they become more alert, just making sure that everyone's okay. I've seen that happen in spaces where there's caregivers and children and I think it's a beautiful addition to the space, and being able to make space for that and to honor that is really important. One thing that BYP100 has done to have intentionality around this is to ensure that when we have meetings we feed each other, we check in before we get started with any of the nuts and bolts of the meetings, we make sure that there is something for the children to do. Folks will take turns and volunteer to care for the children, to color and play with the children or do some type of activity, and that's something that's been built into the culture. I'm also encouraged by other organizations that are committed to children and families and offer things like books and breakfast, arts activities, and liberation circles that are children geared, and also organizers who are having their children lead meetings. Giving children full autonomy and voice in the space and honoring their ability to weigh in on these things that we sometimes feel are so large and that we have to handle as adults, but children are able to really see things just as they are, and they have a level of honesty and frankness that is needed in our spaces because we can get mired down in our analysis.

"Children are able to really see things just as they are."
—JOHNAÉ STRONG

"Children are really great at naming things for what they are and also for very deep optimism. I think the more that we can incorporate these things into our physical and emotional space, it allows us to be more compassionate, more human, more honest and accountable. There's just so many gifts that come from having caregivers and children in the space. I'm definitely still thinking through: How do we make this more essential and part of our work?"

Pain and Possibility

"In my work against state violence, I can feel the oppression, I can feel the pain, and yet I also feel the community physically around me, and I feel the spirit of my ancestors who've gone through this same system of oppression, and in some ways it fortifies me and makes me that much more intent on my goal or vision to stand in our right, to stand in our pursuit of justice and liberation.

"That is a part of this whole larger narrative that is about both the pain and the joy. When I think about my children, I am always optimistic. As a mother, I'm always joyful first, but I never distance or turn away from the hard truth. Rather than shying away from it, my son and I talk about everything from police violence to his Blackness, sexuality, and love. Throughout this journey of deep exploration, there's nothing that I shied away from because I want to hold the complexity of both pain and joy. Both good and bad. When you're dedicating your life to large goals and vision for changing the world, you're going to have to go with the ebb and flow. I just try to remain grateful for all of it."

Return to BYP100's *Black Joy Experience* and listen again to "I Love Being Black." Write an affirmation statement describing five things you love about your Blackness. By now, that affirmation should be integrated into your daily routine. Now it's time to double down on it—in community and movement. As Johnaé shares, there is something powerful to chant and affirm Blackness in community with other Black folks who are committed to Black Liberation.

Liberated Parenting Strategy

Reflect

Black Liberation is intrinsically linked to multiple movement causes. Whether you care about climate change, racial justice, educational rights, reproductive justice, or immigration, each of these movements are connected to the lives of Black people, because we are impacted by all of these issues. Reflect on the issues that you care deeply about. Are the schools in your area lacking resources for students? Are the potholes in the street breaking car axles? Are you living in a food desert, where there is a lack of healthy food options? Do the police harass homeless folks? Spend some time reflecting on what you care deeply about (sometimes that looks like the thing that makes your blood boil every time you see or hear about it). Now that you've found your cause, look for local organizations that you can connect with. Send an email or make a phone call to inquire about volunteer opportunities. Remember that everyone has a role in the fight for liberation. Whatever your unique gift or talent, lend it to the movement.

Practice

As Johnaé shared, having young people involved is powerful in shifting the culture of movements. Young people bring both optimism and vision. Young people have ideas about how the world could be and they are unattached to the way things are. Recall the conversations that both Cecilia and I had with our kids in Section Two about police violence. Both our children at ages six and thirteen had visions about alternatives to violence. Whether it be visiting an organization, attending a community meeting, making a sign for a rally,[9] or participating in a workshop—involving your child in the movement is a personal choice, but one that can help introduce them to activism and advocacy at an early age.

Parenting Communities

Dr. Kim Parker, literacy and equity expert

After listening to the podcast and ordering the first edition of our workbook, Dr. Kim Parker, a mother and literacy activist, reached out to me about an event she was hosting in her Boston community for folks raising Black boys. I was so excited to learn that someone was using the first edition of this guide to hold space and build community with other parents. I happily shared my tools and resources—open source. After her successful event was complete, Dr. Kim joined the podcast to share tips and strategies with folks about how they can build a community of practice in their area. Check out this excerpt:

It Takes a Village

"I knew that I didn't want to do parenting alone. I knew I couldn't do it alone. I also knew that the most powerful way to make sure that my son has a really positive racial identity, and is secure in his Blackness and who he is, was to develop a peer group. I went in search of other Black families and families of Black boys. I already knew some of them and I said we're just going to have this event to celebrate Black boys. The ultimate goal was to develop a critical mass of people who were willing to show up once or twice a month for play groups, for educational events, for talking to each other about parenting Black boys and all the things that come along with it. To build our own intentional community of support for our Black boys, because I knew too well that Boston can be a really lonely and isolating place for people of color. We wanted it to be a queer-affirming space as well and those spaces didn't exist.

"I cohosted the event with one of my best friends, Shauna Thomas. We said we're going to create what we want. If it's just the two of us—Shauna with her grandson and me with my son—then we'll just have a one-on-one playdate and a good lunch and call it a day. But twenty people showed up! It was great because people were so interested. There is such a need for things like that. I just had an idea. I told it to Shauna and she came on board and we decided we're just going to aim for a group of people to come together to create a peer group for our boys.

> "That's been my driving goal: to get people together in a safe place."
> —KIM PARKER

"I'm also sort of guided by the work of my mentor, Dr. Theresa Perry, who would talk to me about how once a week, she, her daughter, and her daughter's classmates would all get together for Sunday brunch to have community. I was like, I want that for my son. I want that for my community. That's been my driving goal: to get people together in a safe place. I feel like when I'm in mixed spaces that I find myself getting uptight—worried that my son might be perceived as something he's not. It wasn't like that in this playdate. We all have Black boys. They were being boys who are rowdy sometimes and they like to be loud and they like to be carefree, and we wanted to give them space to do that. Oftentimes, people would say that their son is the only Black boy in a group. It was just nice to be able to see all of these beautiful Black children playing. We had this intergenerational group of boys which is really fun—from twenty-two months old up to a fifteen-year-old boy."

Plan and Resources

"I was type A while planning this gathering—I was creating a plan, agenda, goals, etc. Shauna asked me, 'Don't you think you have a little bit too much planned? People are going to be happy to just be together and that their can kids play. So while this is great to have this plan, don't be heartbroken if it doesn't happen.'

"When the gathering started, we ate, then we talked about what parenting for liberation is, then we discussed some of the things that get in our way. What came up a lot was fear. Many people are afraid—we are treading a really narrow line between freedom and fear. I love that Trina has made all of her resources so freely available because I wouldn't have been able to host if I hadn't been able to talk to her. Trina gave us the superhero tool for the kids to make their own superhero shields and think about their superpower. We used her guide, which is fantastic. The activities that she has written about, that are coupled with those podcasts, gave us something to talk about. We did the evaluation she created, so that gave us some good ideas about what we want to do next and let us know if people were willing to host another gathering. The time during our first gathering did get away from us because people just wanted to talk together, of course. We ended the day with a really great poem about Brown boys ['The Bronze Legacy (To a Brown Boy)'] from Effie Lee Newsome, a Black poet."

Collective

"I also told the group that this is not my thing. Sure, we brought these people together, but this is only going to work if we are all invested in it and we make it as we go. I tried to make that clear. It's just a matter of reaching out. It just takes one person to plan the event and people will show up. Then you find your people. My whole philosophy toward everything is just keep practicing and learn by doing. That's what I keep telling myself. For our next one, we're going for a hike because where we live is outdoorsy."

Liberated Parenting Strategy

Reflect

What does community look like in your area? Reflect on Malesha's story in Section One of "being the only one"—what does community look like, not only for your child, but for you as a Black parent? What kind of supports do you need? Parenting is often seen as an individual act—what happens in your home is your business—but as reflected in the story with Mia Birdsong, we have a collective and communal parenting culture. Who is in your Parenting for Liberation village?

Practice

If your Parenting for Liberation village doesn't exist yet—e.g., if you relate to Malesha's story of being the only—it's time for you to build it, as Dr. Kim Parker recommends in this story. All it takes is having an idea and moving on it—but you have the additional support of Parenting for Liberation. There are facilitation tools in the back of this book for you to use to host your first parenting circle. It doesn't have to be high pressure. Learn from Kim's cohost Shauna, who said, "All parents really want to do is be together and have a safe place for their Black children to be free to be themselves." You can take, leave, modify, and/or adapt the facilitation tools in the appendices. You are the expert of your community. You know what is needed. If something doesn't apply discard it, if something resonates use it, if something needs to be tweaked to fit your needs, then by all means—tweak it!

Bonus Practice

We at Parenting for Liberation would love to know if you do hold space with folks for a liberated parenting session. If you do, please let us know—share highlights, photos, learnings with us via email and/or via social media using the hashtag #ParentingforLiberation. If you're interested, we'd love to highlight the story of your community on the podcast.

Conclusion

I n the words of the late great Black queer feminist Audre Lorde, "Raising Black children . . . in the mouth of a racist, sexist, suicidal dragon is perilous and chancy. If they cannot love and resist at the same time, they will probably not survive." This quote has been grounding for me as a parent shifting from fear to liberation. For too long, I was only practicing resistance. But in all of my fighting, resisting, and protecting, I eventually realized that I had been blocking my own heart; my hands had not been open to nourish and nurture my children, nor myself. I saw more clearly that I had been parenting from fear. I knew that I must transition from parenting for protection to parenting for liberation, which at its core is love and resistance.

Section One: (Re)connection to Self

The first person I must love is myself. Parenting for Liberation has been a journey to self-love for me as a parent while inviting other parents to have grace and compassion for themselves. As the stories in this section reflect, parenting can be traumatic (Story 1: Breaking Apart as a

Parent) and at times can reopen childhood wounds of feeling unloved (Story 2: Shifting Away from Tough Love), feeling unsafe in our homes (Story 3: Black Fatherhood), or feeling isolated (Story 4: Finding a Village). To support parents in reconnecting with their inner self, Parenting for Liberation hosts gatherings centered on self-care and healing like our Self-Care Sunday—a space dedicated to supporting Black parents in healing, relaxing, and connecting. Our grounding quote for Self-Care Sunday is by none other than Audre Lorde, who said, "Caring for myself is not self-indulgence, it is self-preservation, and that is an act of political warfare." In a world that teaches us to not take care of ourselves, it is revolutionary and healing when we do create the space to do so. We encourage folks to get creative (Story 5: Watering Your Creativity) and offer several self-love/self-care stations such as affirmations, foot soaks, crystals, reiki massages, journaling and reflection, herbal teas, reading nooks, tinctures and sprays, and more. Offered in a relaxing home environment, Black parents are provided space to unwind and connect with one another as we disconnect from the psychological trauma of systemic racism. At Parenting for Liberation, we understand how detrimental the United States can be for Black parents, so we create a peer space where Black parents can decompress, share, and reflect on the impacts of systemic racism on our parenting and exchange strategies about the ways that we can interrupt and heal.

Another gathering we host to reconnect with self is Mothering Ourselves. When we hosted our inaugural Self-Care Sunday event, the attendees provided feedback that "self-care" is at times an isolating experience. What Black parents really need is community. As a result, Parenting for Liberation hosted "community care convenings" to test how centering a Black community care approach to parenting Black children can interrupt the effects of post-traumatic slave syndrome. By intentionally shifting to collective parenting, returning to our ancestral roots of interdependence, and practicing the popular African proverb "It takes a village to raise a child," we interrupt the effects of white supremacy, and Black parents unite to collectively heal on their own behalf, on behalf of their families and communities, to improve our collective quality of life. During our Mothering Ourselves event, we gathered around a healing table filled with ingredients to make body scrubs—oils, essential oils, fresh herbs, and exfoliants—then Black mamas uplifted each other by providing a pampering touch. When we invest in one another, we contribute to a world of Black liberated parents who can show up whole for their children.

Section Two: (Re)connection to Our Children

In addition to parent-specific spaces, Parenting for Liberation also hosts parent-child gatherings, where parents can practice liberated parenting approaches with the support of other parents. For example, during our Black Friday event, parents had a safe space to reflect on their joys and struggles of raising "carefree Black children" and exchange liberated parenting strategies. Parents shared liberated parenting ideas around open communication (Story 6: Family Practices), family structures around rules and discipline (Story 7: Shifting from Rules to Agreements), and how to have age-appropriate conversations with children around sex (Story 8: Conversations about Sex[uality] and Consent), oppression (Story 9: Conversations about History and Oppression, and Story 10: Underground Railroad Museum), and state violence (Story 11: Kitchen Convos and Story 12: No More Police). Simultaneously, the children engaged in a related and age-appropriate arts-and-crafts activity of making superhero capes while discussing their favorite superheroes and learning about hidden heroes of African descent. The gathering closed with the children and parents reunited in an interactive activity, where the children proudly modeled their superhero costumes, and shared their own super powers to their freest and most liberated selves. The parents supported their children by naming liberated parenting practices they would commit to support and cultivate their little superhero.

Section Three: (Re)connection to Community

Moving beyond individual nuclear family structures, Parenting for Liberation hosts community events, presents at conferences, and facilitates workshops as a community building strategy to return to our ancestral roots of raising children in a village (Story 13: Expansive Family Community). This December, we hosted a community Kwanzaa celebration, bringing together one hundred and fifty Black families in South Los Angeles to learn the history, teaching, and celebration of Kwanzaa—and provide Black families with the information and materials to practice Kwanzaa at home from December 26 to January 1. While there are a multitude of ways to celebrate Kwanzaa, families joined us in pouring libations, honoring our ancestors, and coming together through song, dance, African drums, storytelling, spoken word, kids tribal African face-painting, arts and crafts activities, and more. Kwanzaa is not a religious holiday, thus we invited community members of different faiths to participate and practice their traditions of singing Negro spirituals to Nation of Islam drills (Story 14: Communities of Faith). Kwanzaa is a Pan-African holiday, encouraging descendants of the African diaspora to have a global mindset and connect to the Motherland (Story 15: Global Communities). In addition to hosting spaces, Parenting for Liberation facilitates workshops such as our three-week parenting workshop series designed for Black parents to unlearn old ways of parenting and shift to new alternatives to raise healthy, happy, and free children. Using storytelling and art-making as a way for them to tell their own stories—past, present, and future—and explore how their lived experiences can become powerful pathways for healing and liberation. We have facilitated this series at a California women's prison and also in schools (see Stories

16–18 on school communities) such as Thomas Riley High School in Watts, California, with pregnant and parenting teen moms. Regardless of where we are invited, Parenting for Liberation centers the needs of Black parents in movement spaces (Story 19: Movement Communities), such as hosting the Caregiver Track at the Allied Media Conference in 2016, being a catalytic agent of Family Programming with Move to End Violence, to my Wisdom Keeper role holding space for caregivers at Black Love Convergence 2020.

While these are things that I have offered through Parenting for Liberation, I know that similar to raising a child in a village, Parenting for Liberation needs to be nurtured in a village. I have an interest in working with a diverse group of parents, from parents in prisons to parents who are artists and activists and educators, single parents, nonbiological parents, and parents across the gender spectrum (male, female, trans, gender-nonconforming). I hope to have Parenting for Liberation hubs nationwide, engagement in communities of practice (Story 20: Parenting Communities) using a shared leadership approach to harness our collective wisdom, resiliency, and power. Informed by the lessons learned and best practices curated virtually, the communities of practice will be a power base of liberated parents. My ultimate goal is bringing liberated Black parents together as a powerful network to strategize how to advocate for social change and fight for a world where our children can be liberated. Will you join me?

Notes

1. Rochaun Meadows-Fernandez, "After Charlottesville: We Need to Start 'Spoiling' Our Black Children," *Washington Post*, August 15, 2017, https://www.washingtonpost.com/news/parenting/wp/2017/08/15/we-need-to-start-spoiling-our-black-children/.

2. Rochaun Meadows-Fernandez, "'Spoiling' Black Babies: Moms Share Their Stories," *Washington Post*, August 28, 2017, https://www.washingtonpost.com/news/parenting/wp/2017/08/28/spoiling-black-babies-moms-share-their-stories/.

3. Jo Jones and William D. Mosher, "Fathers' Involvement with Their Children: United States, 2006–2010," *National Health Statistics Reports* 71, US Department of Health and Human Services, Centers for Disease Control and Prevention National Center for Health Statistics, December 20, 2013, http://www.cdc.gov/nchs/data/nhsr/nhsr071.pdf.

4. *Essence*, "Black Girls Draw: Jena Holliday Is Proving Black Motherhood Is a Work of Art," November 16, 2017, http://www.url.com.https://www.essence.com/culture/black-girls-draw-jena-holliday-black-motherhood-video.

5. Cathy Malchiodi, "Drawing a Picture of Health: An Art Therapy Guide," *Psychology Today*, March 29, 2017, https://www.psychologytoday.com/us/blog/arts-and-health/201703/drawing-picture-health-art-therapy-guide.

6. American Psychological Association, APA Working Group on Stress and Health Disparities, *Stress and Health Disparities: Contexts, Mechanisms, and Interventions among Racial/Ethnic Minority and Low-Socioeconomic Status Populations*, 2017, http://www.apa.org/pi/health-disparities/resources/stress-report.aspx.

7. Valerie Strauss, "Implicit Racial Bias Causes Black Boys to Be Disciplined at School More Than Whites, Federal Report Finds," *Washington Post*, April 5, 2018. https://www.washingtonpost.com/news/answer-sheet/wp/2018/04/05/implicit-racial-bias-causes-black-boys-to-be-disciplined-at-school-more-than-whites-federal-report-finds/.

8. Stephanie Keeney Parks, "How Racism Impacts Black Kids with Autism: From the Clinic to the Classroom," Speak Up United Parents, August 3, 2018. http://www.url.com.http://speakupparents.org/blog/2018/8/2/how-racism-impacts-black-kids-with-autism-from-the-clinic-to-the-classroom.

9. For a great resource on protesting with your kids, see Jenn Sutherland-Miller, "Activist Mama's Guide to Taking Kids to a March," Medium, January 11, 2017, https://medium.com/jenn-lately/activist-mamas-guide-to-taking-kids-to-a-march-ff5a56340a86.

Glossary

Advocacy: Public support for or recommendation of a particular cause or policy; the profession or work of a legal advocate.

African diaspora: The African diaspora consists of the worldwide collection of communities descended from native Africans or Africa's peoples, predominantly in the Americas.

Black Liberation: Black Liberation focuses on African Americans being liberated from all forms of bondage and injustice—social, political, economic, etc. The Black Liberation movement desired self-determination for the Black community's control of its own organizations, institutions, resources, and land. Some key movements for Black Liberation include the Student Nonviolent Coordinating Committee, the League of Revolutionary Black Workers, the Black Panther Party, and Black Lives Matter.

Classism: Individual prejudice and systemic discrimination against individuals or groups on the basis of their social class or perceived social class. Classism ranks people according to economic status, family lineage, job status, level of education; and places low or working-class status as inferior to upper class.

Colonialism: The policy or practice of politically controlling, occupying, and exploiting another country economically and culturally. The United States was colonized by Great Britain, but colonization has been perpetrated on every continent. Colonialism is a social and cultural system that relies on unbalanced power relationships and unequal distribution of resources favoring the colonizers over the people who are indigenous to the the occupied land.

Decolonization: The undoing of colonialism and imperialism; putting power and distribution of resources back in the favor of people who are indigenous to the occupied land.

Framily: An expanded idea of family that includes close friends.

Gender-nonconforming, genderqueer, or nonbinary: Any gender that does not fit into the constructed male and female binary.

Historical trauma: A collective complex trauma inflicted on a group of people who share a specific group identity or affiliation—ethnicity, nationality, and/or religion. It is the legacy of numerous traumatic events a community experiences over generations and encompasses the psychological and social responses to such events.

Intergenerational trauma: Trauma that is transferred from the first generation of trauma survivors to the second and further generations of offspring of the survivors via complex post-traumatic stress disorder mechanisms. While the trauma itself is not passed on, the symptoms of surviving trauma (e.g., post-traumatic stress, coping mechanisms, survival strategies) can be passed on. Scientific data has shown that this trauma is not only passed on from behavior but can also be passed down through DNA and epigenetics.

Internalized oppression: Attitude that leads people who are the target of one form of oppression to believe the negative messages against their group and sometimes end up acting against their own self-interests.

Intersectionality: Coined by academic Kimberlé Crenshaw, this term focuses on the ways our collective identities across sex, gender, race, ethnicity, nationality/citizenship status, religion, class, age, size, ability, and other categories of difference and inequality affect our lives, including what we experience, how we act, how others act toward us, and what we think. It's a way to describe the interconnected nature of social categorizations (e.g., race, class, gender, sexuality) as they apply to a given individual or group; regarded as creating overlapping and interdependent systems of discrimination or disadvantage.

Islamophobia: The fear, hatred of, or prejudice against the Islamic religion or Muslims generally, especially when seen as a geopolitical force or the source of terrorism.

LGBTQIA+: A term that includes and makes visible lesbian, gay, bisexual, transgender, intersex, and asexual people within the queer community.

Liberation: The act of setting someone free from imprisonment, slavery, or oppression; release. To be free from limits on thoughts or behaviors.

Marginalize: To treat (a person, group, or concept) as insignificant or peripheral.

Microaggression: A statement, action, or incident regarded as an instance of indirect, subtle, or unintentional discrimination against members of marginalized and/or targeted groups based on race, sex, gender identity, sexuality, ethnicity, nationality, citizenship status, relationship status, religion, visible or invisible ability, size, age, and additional categories subjected to systems of inequality.

Movement / movement building: A group of people with a shared purpose to create change together by advancing social, political, and economic justice for marginalized groups. Some strategies for movement building may include advocacy, protests, media outreach, legal action, and research.

Oppression: A situation in which people are governed by an authority or power in an unfair and cruel way and prevented from having opportunities and freedom.

Othering: To view or treat a person or group of people as intrinsically different from and alien to oneself.

Parenting: The act of nurturing life. In this context, parenting can happen via any caregiver or guardian of children and youth, including nonbiological caregivers. We are holding parenting and caregiving in the most expansive way, acknowledging the multitude of folks who nurture children and youth including foster parents, godparents, grandparents, etc.

Post-Traumatic Slave Syndrome (PTSS): A theory that explains the impact of US chattel slavery on African Americans. It explains how the adaptive survival behaviors in African American communities throughout the United States and the diaspora is a result of multigenerational oppression of Africans and their descendants.

Queer/transphobia: Dislike, hate toward, fear of, or prejudice against LGBQTIA+ people; systemic discrimination and violence against nonheterosexual people.

Racism: Individual and systemic discrimination or antagonism directed against someone or a social group because of their race, ethnicity, color, and/or national origin; based on the white-supremacist belief that whiteness is superior.

School-to-prison pipeline: In the United States, the school-to-prison pipeline, also known as the school-to-prison link or the schoolhouse-to-jailhouse track, is the disproportionate tendency of minors and young adults of color to become incarcerated because of increasingly harsh school and municipal policies. The disciplinary policies and practices that create an environment for the US school-to-prison link to occur disproportionately affect Black (in addition to Latinx and differently abled) students, which is later reflected in the rates of incarceration.

Sexism: Prejudice, stereotyping, or discrimination, typically against women, on the basis of sex.

Storytelling: Sharing experiences and/or stories; grounded in our ancestors' oral traditions of teaching and learning.

Trauma: Trauma occurs when a person is overwhelmed by a deeply distressing or disturbing experience, event, or circumstance and responds with intense fear, horror, and helplessness.

Xenophobia: The fear and distrust of that which is perceived to be foreign or strange; can manifest itself in suspicion of the activities of others, and a desire to eliminate their presence to secure a presumed purity and may relate to a fear of losing national, ethnic, or racial identity.

Hosting a #LiberatedParent Gathering

Are you interested in creating your own parenting circle? In this section, there are three resources for you to use as you begin. First, I've included a template with reflection questions you may want to consider as you plan the event. Following this are two agendas: a sample one from Parenting for Liberation and then a real-world example Dr. Kim Parker from Story 20 used. As you can see from these two agendas, you can adapt them to fit the unique needs of your own community.

Template for Hosting a Gathering and Reflection Questions

Logistics:

Goal/Purpose/Outcome: Reflect on why you want to bring people together. What do you hope to get out of this gathering? What will be the takeaway for the folks who attend?

Date and Time: Is the date and time convenient for parents? Check for competing events and holidays.

Location: Is the location centrally located? Can folks on public transportation access the venue? Is the space conducive to Black families (i.e., Black owned)? Is the venue accessible for folks with disabilities? Is the building child friendly? Is there space for breakout sessions if needed?

Setup:

Food and Drinks: Are there any special dietary needs/restrictions? Is the caterer a Black-owned business?

Tables and Chairs: How do you want your setup organized (in a circle to promote dialogue)? Is there a separate space for kids to play? Will there be music? What supplies are needed?

Support: Do you have a caregiver to support the children?

Agenda:

Opening: This sets the tone for the overall event—how will you open the space?

Introductions: Invite folks into the conversation and get to know one another as quickly as possible through introductions.

Children's Session: Who is leading the children's space? How are you celebrating Blackness with the children? What arts and crafts activities are you using to support their sense of liberation? What readings are you sharing?

Parents' Session: Parents need space to connect and share. How do you create a safe space for Black parents to share their deepest fears and highest accomplishments as parents? Sometimes the host has to share their truths first and practice vulnerability as a model so others can engage—how do you get parents to open up?

Collective Close: What are powerful ways to close the space that uplift folks and celebrate the time you spent together? Is it a collective chant? A poem or song? Or perhaps a closing prompt (one word to describe how you feel)?

Next Steps/Follow-Up: What are next steps? Is there an invitation to continue this group? Is there an evaluation to get feedback on the attendees' experience?

Sample Agenda for Concurrent Parent/Child(ren) Workshops

Shared by Parenting for Liberation

Parent/Main Room Setup:

- ○ Two food/drinks tables.
- ○ One registration table (sign-in, release, raffle ticket, name tags).
- ○ One sales table.
- ○ Banner/decorations uplifting Blackness.
- ○ Music: Parenting for Liberation playlist and BYP100's *Black Joy Experience*.
- ○ Photo booth props.
- ○ Chairs arranged in a circle for story circle.
- ○ Tables and chairs along the perimeter for eating.

ACTIVITY:	Opening Joint Session for Parents and Children
TIME:	30 minutes
DESCRIPTION:	○ Welcoming and grounding. ○ Introductions: Each person introduces themselves and their family. ○ Overview of Agenda.
MATERIALS:	Agenda

ACTIVITY:	**Kids' Breakout Session**
	(happens concurrently with Parents' Breakout Session)
TIME:	45 minutes
DESCRIPTION:	Check-in (led by Youth Leaders)

- What is your name?
- Who is your favorite superhero?
- What superpower does he/she possess?
- Who are heroes in your life?

Discussion: Help kids understand that heroes are not only superheroes but everyday people who stand up for what is right or help someone in need.

Hidden Heroes in Our History—Tips: I recommend researching local heroes in your area. Urban Intellectuals has multiple Black History Flashcard decks. Also Jamia Wilson's book *Young, Gifted and Black* has over 52 Black leaders. Here are some examples: Shirley Chisholm; Nina Simone; Ruby Bridges; Malcolm X; Martin Luther King Jr.; Angela Davis; Frederick Douglass; James Baldwin; Huey P. Newton; Claudette Colvin.

Superhero Activity:
- Design superhero capes and/or masks.
- Create superhero shield.

MATERIALS:	Superhero capes; masks; art supplies such as markers, paint, stickers, etc.

ACTIVITY:	**Parents' Breakout Session**
	(happens concurrently with Kids' Breakout Session)
TIME:	45 minutes
DESCRIPTION:	○ Introduce Parenting for Liberation.
	○ Share story of shifting from fear to liberation.
	○ Share current activities—podcast, guide.
	○ Go through one page activity from guide.
MATERIALS:	*Parenting for Liberation*

ACTIVITY:	Parents' and Kids' Joint Session
TIME:	15 minutes
DESCRIPTION:	Runway Showcased by Children ○ Kids arrive in parent space for runway. ○ Youth Leaders introduce kids and their superpower (*Rip the Runway* style). ○ Parents encourage and cheer for all kids.
MATERIALS:	Chairs; runway

ACTIVITY:	**Mural Wall**
TIME:	15 minutes
DESCRIPTION:	Children share their superpower (written on star) and parents will make commitments on a shift they can make to help support their child(ren) in cultivating that superpower (e.g., Terrence's superpower is teleportation; Trina commits to support his ability to move without restrictions such as allowing him to play outside without constant supervision).

ACTIVITY:	**Closing Chant (by Assata Shakur)**
TIME:	10 minutes
DESCRIPTION:	"It is our duty to fight for our freedom. It is our duty to win. We must love each other and support each other. We have nothing to lose but our chains."

Free, Whole, and Happy Black Boys
Kick-Off Brunch Agenda

February 24, 2018, 11:00 a.m.–1:00 p.m.,
Make Shift Boston

Materials:
Clip boards; serving utensils, paper goods; big paper; markers for big paper; crayons; superhero handout; handout from *Parenting for Liberation*; *Parenting for Liberation*; survey; Effie Lee Newsome's poem "The Bronze Legacy (To a Brown Boy)"

Welcome and Introductions (11:00–11:45 a.m.)

(Make sure you have a sign-up sheet for the mailing list)

- ○ Appreciation and gratitude for attending.
- ○ Each person introduces self and family (kids' names and ages) and what brings them out today.
- ○ Introduce Parenting for Liberation. Find a quote from Trina to frame this.
- ○ Go through one page activity from book.
- ○ Conversations depending on size of group (whole group or small groups).
- ○ Read aloud from *Crown: An Ode to the Fresh Cut* by Derrick Barnes.

Mingling, Quick Energizer: Big Paper Visioning (11:45 a.m.–12:00 p.m.)

What do we want this group to be and become?

Prompts:
- ○ What does parenting for liberation mean for you and your family?
- ○ How do you practice liberation on a day-to-day basis?
- ○ What do you love about your Black boy?
- ○ What are your hopes and dreams for this group?
- ○ Resources.
- ○ Questions.

Children's Breakout Session: Superheroes and Superpowers (12:00–12:30 p.m.)

Check-in with children:
- ○ What is your name and who is your favorite superhero?
- ○ What superpower does he/she possess?
- ○ Who are heroes in your life?

Discussion: Help kids understand that heroes are not only superheroes but everyday people who stand up for what is right or help someone in need. Hidden heroes in our history:

- ○ Shirley Chisholm
- ○ Nina Simone
- ○ Ruby Bridges
- ○ Malcolm X
- ○ Rosa Parks
- ○ Martin Luther King Jr.

You are ALL Superheroes! Families complete superhero picture and share at end of session.

Closing and Next Steps (12:30–12:45 p.m.)

Monthly social gatherings and educational outings; planning group? Survey Reminders: Sign up for the mailing list!

Parenting for Liberation podcast and guide: listen and purchase!

Closing Circle: One Word (12:45–1:00 p.m.)
Closing Poem: "The Bronze Legacy (To a Brown Boy)" by Effie Lee Newsome

Conclude and Clean Up: Expressions of Gratitude! (1:00 p.m.)

Resources for Further Reading

All About Love: New Visions by bell hooks

Between the World and Me by Ta-Nehisi Coates

The Chicana M(other)work Anthology by Cecilia Caballero,
    Yvette Martínez-Vu, Judith Pérez-Torres, Michelle Téllez,
    and Christine Vega

*The Deepest Well: Healing the Long-Term Effects of Childhood
    Adversity* by Nadine Burke Harris

The Fire Next Time by James Baldwin

*The Healing Wisdom of Africa: Finding Life Purpose Through Nature,
    Ritual, and Community* by Malidoma Patrice Somé

Letters to My Black Sons: Raising Boys in a Post-Racial America by
    Karsonya Wise Whitehead

*My Brown Baby: On the Joys and Challenges of Raising African
    American Children* by Denene Millner

*My Grandmother's Hands: Racialized Trauma and the Pathway to
    Mending Our Hearts and Bodies* by Resmaa Menakem

*Post Traumatic Slave Syndrome: America's Legacy of Enduring Injury
    and Healing* by Joy DeGruy

Revolutionary Mothering: Love on the Front Lines by Alexis Pauline
Gumbs, China Martens, and Mai'a Williams

Rise Up Singing: Black Women Writers on Motherhood edited by
Cecelie Berry

Spare the Kids: Why Whupping Children Won't Save Black America by
Stacey Patton

*This Is How We Survive: Revolutionary Mothering, War, and Exile in the
21st Century* by Mai'a Williams

Today I Affirm: A Journal That Nurtures Self-Care by Alexandra Elle

Toni Morrison and Motherhood: A Politics of the Heart by Andrea
O'Reilly

*We Can Speak for Ourselves: Parent Involvement and Ideologies of
Black Mothers in Chicago* by Billye Sankofa Waters

We Live for the We: The Political Power of Black Motherhood by
Dani McClain

*What Mama Couldn't Tell Us About Love: Healing the Emotional
Legacy of Racism by Celebrating Our Light* by Brenda Lane
Richardson and Brenda Wade

When They Call You a Terrorist: A Black Lives Matter Memoir by
Patrisse Khan-Cullors and asha bandele

*Why Are All the Black Kids Sitting Together in the Cafeteria?: And
Other Conversations About Race* by Beverly Daniel Tatum

Acknowledgments

Much gratitude and appreciation for all the amazing Black parents who shared their stories with me. Your offerings were not only investments in Parenting for Liberation as an organization but in me as a parent and in my children. Thank you to Mia Birdsong, Cecilia Caballero, Jena Holliday, Neil Irvin, Tiffany Lanoix, Ida McCrae, A. Rochaun Meadows-Fernandez, Monalisa Oluko Diallo, Dr. Kim Parker, Dia Penning, Ignacio Rivera, Jacqueline Roebuck Sakho, Mikala Streeter, Johnaé Strong, Malesha Taylor, and Mai'a Williams for sowing seeds of liberation within me and many other Black parents.

Thank you to the Feminist Press team—led by my dear friend and sister Jamia Wilson, who is committed to making sure Black children see themselves on the page—for helping bring this book to life. Thanks to the teams at the NoVo Foundation and Move to End Violence for investing in my leadership and vision as a Movement Maker. (In South Africa, Monica asked what would I do if I were ten times bolder—welp, this book is it!)

Thanks to my village that nurtured me and supported me through this writing process. To my family, who shows up and shows out at every

P4L function: My daddy, who proudly wore his P4L shirt every time I saw him and who taught me so much with his own PhD in the school of hard knocks. Thank you for every lesson and nugget of wisdom you provided me as a Black girl from the hood, lessons about sexism through hip hop, teaching me to raise my fist high for Black Power, and always reminding me of my value as a Black woman. Thank you for liberating me so that I can support the liberation of my children and others. I love and miss you, Daddy.

My mama, who taught me to be a lifelong learner and reader, and always said "parenting doesn't come with a manual" (well, Mama, I created one!); and to my sisters, brothers, Granny, and Papa, thank you for being my coparenting village as liberated aunts, uncles, and grandparents to my children. To my sister-friend Lesli, thank you for seeing me and hearing me, and for reflecting back on paper what you witness. To my husband, Andrew, thank you for coparenting with me, and picking up my slack with the kids while I traveled and stayed up late on writing binges.

Lastly thanks to the two beings who give me the honorable role of parent—my children, Terrence and Ariyah. Thank you for pushing me, challenging me, and holding me accountable to live my values. Thank you for embodying liberation and showing me what is possible when Black boys live out loud with joy and Black girls practice their magic.

The Feminist Press publishes books that
ignite movements and social transformation.
Celebrating our legacy, we lift up insurgent
and marginalized voices from around the
world to build a more just future.

See our complete list of books at
feministpress.org

THE FEMINIST PRESS
AT THE CITY UNIVERSITY OF NEW YORK
FEMINISTPRESS.ORG